STRATEGIES AGAINST POVERTY

BY THE SAME AUTHOR

Up From Poverty (WITH HERMINE POPPER)
Social Class and Social Policy (WITH S. M. MILLER)
The Culturally Deprived Child

STRATEGIES AGAINST

POVERTY

by Frank Riessman

 RANDOM HOUSE / NEW YORK

ACKNOWLEDGMENTS

Some of the chapters in this book were written in collaboration with various colleagues; a number have appeared as articles, and I should like to thank my co-authors, as well as several publishers, for permission to reprint.

"The Myth of Saul Alinsky" (July-August 1967) and "The Moynihan Report" (March-April 1966) originally appeared in *Dissent*. "The Strategy of Style" was first published in the *Teachers College Record* (March 1964); "Digging 'The Man's' Language," by Frank Riessman and Frank Alberts, *Saturday Review*, September 17, 1966. For the chapter entitled "A New Education Strategy," my collaborator was Lita Paniagua, Associate Research Scientist, New Careers Training Laboratory. The section on the Neighborhood Service Center in Chapter VIII first appeared in the *American Journal of Psychiatry*, Vol. 123, May 1967, pp. 1408-1413, co-author, Emanuel Hallowitz, M.S.W., of the Lincoln Hospital Mental Health Services. "Training the Nonprofessional" is reprinted from the *Community Mental Health Journal*, Vol. 3, No. 2, 1967. Chapter X, "Birth Control, Culture, and the Poor," by Catherine Kohler Riessman, was first published in the *American Journal of Orthopsychiatry*, Vol. 38, No. 4, July 1968, copyright, the American Orthopsychiatric Association, Inc., reproduced by permission.

I should like particularly to thank Florence Haussamen, writer-consultant on the staff of the New Careers Development Center, for her helpful editing on the final manuscript.

To the Staff of

the NEW CAREERS DEVELOPMENT CENTER
and the NEW CAREERS TRAINING LABORATORY

INTRODUCTION

The recognition that there was great poverty in the United States came in 1962, partly brought about by the thrust of the civil rights movement. A spate of books starting with Michael Harrington's *The Other America* presaged the new concern with a poverty that gripped a fifth of the nation. Also in 1962 Congress passed the Manpower Development Training Act, which provided training allowances and a training program for the unemployed.

As reflected in Harrington, Patricia Sexton, James B. Conant, and others, the initial concern about poverty was largely oriented toward illuminating the problem. Harrington showed that the poor were cycled into poverty, and had little opportunity for escaping it. It became increasingly clear that most of the services provided to the poor were not merely deficient, but functioned as antiservices. For example, the school system not only failed to educate large masses of children, but, in addition, it alienated youngsters from education, leading to what Edgar Friedenberg termed the "ideology of school withdrawal" (the dropout-kickout syndrome). Schools were actually producing mindlessness, and a basically anti-intellectual bias. Similarly, the welfare system was not assisting poor people to gain coping skills, to regain dignity, to function in the system and to move out of poverty—rather, it helped people remain within the cycle of poverty, making it essentially impossible for them to work and maintain an income. In addition, welfare regulations limited them in countless ways—beyond the restrictions imposed by poverty itself.

The protection system of the society is notable for its failure to protect the areas of the poor and the ghetto. The latter has two complaints about the police: (1) that it discriminates, and (2) that it does not protect, but permits random lawlessness within the neighborhoods of the poor.

The health system not only fails to provide the necessary health care for large numbers of people, but it actually drives people away from utilizing available health services by furnishing them in a poorly organized, inhumane, bureaucratic fashion. That the poor are "medically deprived," resulted in the myth that they were victims of the "culture of poverty," unable to plan for their future health—the natural outgrowth of the antiservice provided.

It was natural to be concerned about ways of dealing with this newly illuminated poverty syndrome and so there emerged various strategies for removing or reducing it. Many of these strategies were expressed in embryonic form in a program which began in 1962 as an antidelinquency experiment, Mobilization for Youth, operating on the Lower East Side in New York City.* MFY was the forerunner of most of the antipoverty strategies that were later embodied in the Economic Opportunity Act. MFY started neighborhood storefronts to serve as advocates for the poor; it employed indigenous nonprofessionals to work as school-community coordinators, case aides; it developed a homeworker helper program in the schools; it started a legal unit for testing aspects of the welfare laws. And MFY ultimately became a base for the welfare rights movement in New York City.

The Ford Foundation sponsored projects in fourteen "great" cities directed toward improving education for the disadvantaged. The emphasis on the preschool strategy, later reflected in Operation Headstart, was originally funded by the Ford Foundation, which sponsored the experimental work of Martin Deutsch.[1] In this same period the activist community-based approach of Saul Alinsky expanded and began to receive national attention.

The Economic Opportunity Act of 1964 focused attention

---

* Funded by the Ford Foundation in combination with a number of government agencies, most especially the Office of Juvenile Delinquency.

[1] For a critique of this strategy, see F. Riessman, "The New Pre-School Mythology; Child-Centered Radicalism," *American Child*, Spring 1966.

on a great variety of antipoverty strategies that were then experimented with by the OEO. These included the residential job-training approach of the Job Corps; a variety of services for the poor such as legal aid, consumer aid, family planning, decentralized neighborhood health approaches, community action involving the participation of the poor, Operation Headstart, the employment of indigenous nonprofessionals in a variety of community-action programs.

Most recent antipoverty legislative approaches have emerged in the field of education: the Vocational Educational Act of 1963, the Higher Education Act (1965), the National Defense Education Act (1965), and the Elementary and Secondary Education Act of 1965. All these acts in various ways are concerned with developing educational strategies for the disadvantaged. The most important new piece of legislation, passed in 1968, is the Education Professions Development Act.

This book analyzes the major antipoverty strategies that have emerged in the 1960's. The first part focuses on three major strategies that are receiving considerable national attention, beginning with the Alinsky conflict model, which is directed toward increasing the power of the poor through developing conflict. It assumes a finite pool of power, with the poor having a limited amount in contrast to the ruling groups. Alinsky attempts to alter this power distribution through producing conflicts and organization.

The second major strategy, the welfare crisis strategy, has been developed by Richard Cloward and Francis Piven. The principal idea is to produce a crisis, or "run," on the welfare system, which might lead the government to grant a guaranteed annual income to all as a way out. The strategy has been strongly connected with the welfare rights movement, but it is possible to view the two as separate entities, because the latter may be an excellent organization for expressing the demands of welfare recipients and insuring that their rights are obtained, without necessarily serving as a strategy for ending their welfare status or removing their poverty.

The third strategy, the New Careers model developed by Arthur Pearl and myself, is directed toward providing an opportunity for poor people to move out of poverty, rather than to become more comfortable in it. The strategy does not require a constituency of poor people remaining poor. It is concerned rather with providing a career ladder for the disadvantaged, who may begin in nonprofessional jobs, requiring few skills, and move up to a career as a professional or an administrator.

Any strategy obviously centers its emphasis on a particular variable or complex of variables, whether power, jobs, participation. The ultimate test of the strategy is whether it affects related variables other than the one it immediately acts upon— that is, its multiplier effect. If an antipoverty strategy acts directly on jobs, does it affect status, self-respect, alienation, participation, family planning, and other poverty-related characteristics, or is its impact narrowly restricted to the one variable it directly affects? A major thesis of this book is that the New Careers strategy has a far greater multiplier effect on the various dimensions of poverty and furthermore that it has additional benefits, or pluses, in that it provides a significant potential for broad institutional change, especially with regard to the reorganization of the education, health, and welfare service systems.

The second half of the book is devoted to more specific strategies in some of the human-service fields—mental health, education, and family planning. Beginning with a critique of the compensatory education strategy and the Moynihan Report, specific countereducational approaches are proposed. The neighborhood service center model is then presented as a significant decentralizing approach for reaching the poor and providing important services for them and with them. This is followed by a mental health strategy for the poor. Finally there is a discussion of family planning, which is seen as a significant antipoverty strategy. This last chapter is contributed by my wife, Catherine Kohler Riessman.

Thus the book attempts to contrast three general antipoverty approaches and proceeds to more specific strategies based in large part on the New Careers model and the utilization of nonprofessionals in decentralized structures.

FRANK RIESSMAN

August 1968

CONTENTS

PART

I

THE MYTH OF
SAUL ALINSKY

One of the most diverting aspects of the new anti-poverty thinking is a one-sided emphasis on conflict and power which is divorced from program and policy. This is not to slight the significance of increasing the power of the poor—but perhaps this power can be more readily expanded by proposals that are meaningful to large segments who can then be organized to demand these programs.

Most poor people are not concerned with power *per se*, but with services, income, immediate needs, education, and the like. Thus it seems more reasonable that they organize to increase their power to have these needs met. An emphasis on power in the abstract or on increasing participation of the poor on committees and antipoverty boards, that ignores specifics and goals, has for obvious reasons interested only a small segment of the poor; if candidates have no program beyond increasing the participation of the poor—which is really much too vague—the people don't know what they are voting for.

Increased power brings dignity and respect. The question at issue is how one develops and builds this power. Moreover, an "against" approach, which the current power theorists stress, also has only limited appeal. It becomes nihilistic, empty, and cynical unless it is connected to specific demands which are based on policy analysis that leads to institutional changes that can produce long-range remedies. The protest-and-power concepts have unbalanced the scales. The need for planning, policy, and theory, including analysis of the American scene and its potential in the 1960's and 1970's, has been grossly underestimated.

It is most fascinating that Saul Alinsky's approach to community organizing is commonly regarded as a radical one and that a number of people with progressive and radical leanings are so strongly attracted to it. However, the Alinsky model neither implies a radical view of society nor calls for radical social change. What, then, are its essential ingredients of social action?[1]

The major goal is to build a powerful neighborhood organization. This organization is to include all elements in the community—the people, the clergy, businessmen's groups, PTA's, service groups, block groups, the "poor."[2] Essentially it is to be a local united front, an organization of organizations, and, like a labor union, it attempts to maintain its status as the sole bargaining agent in the area. The local organization involves at most 2 percent of the people in the community; its purpose is to shift power to itself by taking it away from the

---

[1] See Saul D. Alinsky, *Reveille for Radicals*, Chicago, University of Chicago Press, 1945. Alinsky, "The Urban Immigrant," in T. T. McAvoy, ed., *Roman Catholicism and the American Way of Life*, Notre Dame, Ind., University of Notre Dame Press, 1960. Alinsky, "Citizen Participation and Community Organization in Planning and Urban Renewal." Address to National Association of Housing and Redevelopment Officials, Chicago, January 1962.

[2] See Thomas D. Sherrard and Richard C. Murray, "The Church and Neighborhood Community Organization," *Social Work*, Vol. 10, No. 3, July 1965, pp. 3-14.

existing local groups that are most vulnerable.[3]

Alinsky's model organization is built largely through stirring conflict, "rubbing raw the sores of discontent," attempting to disorganize whatever community organization exists.[4] A continuous state of militancy is emphasized, and demonstrations, pickets, boycotts, direct action, and publicity are stressed in order to involve people in building the organization.

For example, in Alinsky's best-known group—The Woodlawn Organization in Chicago (TWO)—the aim was to expose and stop the exploitation by neighborhood merchants who were overcharging. TWO got the cooperation of Woodlawn residents and community leaders and received a great deal of publicity. TWO also organized tenant groups trying to get slum landlords to repair building-code violations. If the landlords would not comply, TWO called rent strikes and picketed the homes of some landlords in white suburbs.

These are typical activities used all over the country by many different consumer, tenant, and civil rights groups to win specific gains. Alinsky attempts to use these tactics in order to develop local organization and power.

SOCIOTHERAPY FOR THE POOR

Writers like Charles Silberman and Warren Haggstrom have added a sociotherapeutic dimension to the Alinsky model, arguing that militant social action presumably transforms apathetic, dependent, poor people into independent, dignified citizens.[5] Haggstrom believes that poor people need power, not

[3] Nicholas von Hoffman, the principal Alinsky organizer in Woodlawn, wrote: "It is an organization of perhaps two per cent of the people. Those who talk about organizing 'all the people,' or 'the masses,' or 'the great majority of the people,' are talking unrealizable balderdash." "Finding and Making Leaders," Ann Arbor; Students for a Democratic Society, 1964, p. 9.

[4] See Saul Alinsky, "From Citizen Apathy to Participation." Paper presented at the Association of Community Councils of Chicago, October 1957, pp. 4 and 6.

[5] Charles Silberman, *Crisis in Black and White*, New York, Random House, 1964, Chapter 10. (This is essentially the same as "Up from Apathy —The Woodlawn Experiment," *Commentary*, Vol. 37, No. 5, May 1964.) Warren C. Haggstrom, "The Power of the Poor," in *Mental Health of the Poor*, edited by Riessman, Cohen, Pearl. New York, Free Press, 1964, pp. 205-212.

money, and that this power will make them feel able and competent. In discussing the sociotherapeutic implications of the Alinsky model, Sherrard and Murray comment:

> It is assumed that aggression is a natural way for people who have been oppressed, mistreated, exploited or neglected to respond to those who have misused them, and that this [conflict] mode of organization will therefore overcome apathy and sustain participation among those who would not otherwise be willing to expend their energy on any social enterprise.
> It is perhaps assumed that this stance of righteous anger attracts certain kinds of people who seem to require more compelling and intensive involvement than they get attending meetings and engaging in community problem solving. A militant stance of this sort may also encourage the timid who have legitimate complaints and have suffered and have been exploited to come forward and air their grievances. . . . This activity may indeed be therapeutic, if by acting out and giving vent to their hostilities these deprived individuals and groups attain subsequently a more stable and realistic relationship to their institutional environment. However, unless there is accompanying change in their environment such activity may disrupt and further prevent the participants from making a new social adjustment. Any "therapy" must, above all, be realistic and honest at the same time that it raises aspiration and motivation—admittedly a difficult balance to achieve. It is yet to be proved that conflict organization is indeed therapeutic.[6]

WHAT ARE THE LOCAL RESULTS?

Apart from the fact that Alinsky offers no national program directed toward social change, what has he achieved locally through his model? He contends that his Industrial Areas Foundation (IAF) has organized over 2 million people in 44 communities over the last thirty years. However, as Arthur Hillman comments, "Certainly if one out of every 100 people in the population are somehow enrolled or had recently been involved, the whole movement would have been much better

[6] Sherrard and Murray, *op. cit.*, p. 9.

known long before the recent publicity."[7] Alinsky offers no systematic evidence of any kind regarding the numbers of people he has organized. Moreover, it is very difficult even to locate the 44 communities now. A good many of them seem not to have survived for any period of time.

In the better-known communities that Alinsky has organized (or stimulated) —Chelsea in New York City, The Woodlawn Organization in Chicago, FIGHT in Rochester, Back of the Yards in Chicago, the Syracuse Community Action Training Project—there is considerable question as to their effectiveness and achievements. The Chelsea project in New York, organized in the 1940's, which is rarely referred to any more, was a complete fiasco.[8] It ended with great bitterness, no results, and disorganization. The Back of the Yards project in Chicago remains well organized, but has ultimately become anti-Negro. Alinsky resigned from the Syracuse project not long after the going got rough, and the Office of Economic Opportunity (which has funded the organization) required that the project be placed under the umbrella of the city-wide antipoverty agency. Alinsky seemed completely unable to develop tactics to respond to this condition. Moreover, the achievements in the Syracuse project (such as organizing tenants in public housing projects) were probably not any more outstanding than those of the great variety of far less militant community action projects developed through antipoverty funding. For example, the Lincoln Hospital Neighborhood Service Center Program also organized tenants, participated in voter registration campaigns and the welfare rights movement with far less fanfare.[9]

In Rochester the Alinsky-inspired agency called FIGHT has developed an almost completely segregated Negro organization. FIGHT's main demand was for on-the-job training for Negro youngsters in the area. Recently, perhaps as a result of much criticism regarding his localism, Alinsky has been sug-

[7] Personal communication from Arthur Hillman, Director of the National Friends Service Training Center, Chicago, Illinois.

[8] E. C. Parker, "How Chelsea Was Torn Apart," *Christian Century,* February 3, 1960, p. 130.

[9] See Emanuel Hallowitz and Frank Riessman, "The Role of the Indigenous Nonprofessional in a Community Mental Health Neighborhood Service Center Program," *American Journal of Orthopsychiatry,* 1967.

gesting that the Eastman-Kodak issue in Rochester may spread to become a national issue for every Negro ghetto in America and "revive the fading civil rights movement."[10]

There is no question that considerable press attention has been directed toward the Kodak issue and Stokely Carmichael has been introduced to Rochester. The question remains, however, whether it is more of a national newspaper issue than a movement. For example, "the national boycott of Kodak, which Carmichael promised to help organize, turned out to be a complete flop. Picketing scheduled in only nine cities actually occurred in four. At that only a few dozen showed up in New York, Detroit, Chicago and San Francisco and only five to seven in Atlanta."[11]

Perhaps even more relevant is the fact that locally in Rochester anti-Semitism expressed by Reverend Florence, the head of FIGHT, has antagonized supporters. Moreover, Kodak, Xerox, and other firms throughout the nation are involved in providing on-the-job training for "hard-core poor." The demand is not unique to FIGHT, and it is achieving results without the militant rhetoric that characterizes FIGHT. To pretend that there is deep establishment resistance to this program of on-the-job training and that only some militant organization can break this resistance is patently absurd. Reverend Leon Sullivan has developed similar, far more successful projects (Opportunity Industrialization Centers) in Philadelphia and other cities with much less revolutionary rhetoric.

Alinsky's most publicized organization is The Woodlawn Organization, TWO, in Chicago. Countless newspaper and magazine writers have visited this project to bring back glowing reports about the development of dignity in the people of the area, victories over local shopkeepers and slumlords, exciting tactics (truth squads, death watches), and presumably the organization of previously apathetic, uninvolved, hard-core poor people.[12] Various Chicago-based social-scientist observers, however, present quite different reports. Sherrard and Murray,

[10] See Barbara Carter, "The Fight Against Kodak," *The Reporter*, April 27, 1967, pp. 28-31.

[11] *Ibid.*, p. 31.

[12] Articles about Alinsky have appeared in *Harper's, Commentary, The Sunday Times Magazine, The Reporter, Saturday Evening Post, Look, New Republic, Time*, etc.

Arthur Hillman, and Philip Hauser all raise serious questions (see below) regarding the TWO project, and again it must be remarked that Alinsky has no systematic evidence whatsoever to back up the high-order publicity claims which have emerged.[13] Thus, Sherrard and Murray—who live, work, and conduct research in Chicago and along with Hillman have studied The Woodlawn Organization at close hand—seriously question the claim that TWO has reached the most deprived segment of the community. Hillman states: "Various kinds of evidence and the judgment of observers show that TWO's leaders and principal participants are middle class or upwardly mobile lower class persons. They are definitely not the most deprived or depressed."

Sherrard and Murray note in regard to the Chicago projects (and they are referring to all four of Alinsky's groups in Chicago) that "these church-sponsored organizations have introduced a number of persons into political and city-wide prominence, but they have not become city-wide leaders. Organizational preoccupation with local self-interest and hostility toward city-wide institutions severely limits their municipal-leadership potential."

The question has also been raised as to whether pressure on offending merchants and slumlords forces changes that endure for any length of time. Supermarket boycotts by women in various cities in the United States and Toronto probably stimulated the reduction of prices for a short time, but whether these prices will long remain at the new level is an open question. Tenant groups throughout the country, without the organization and funding of Alinsky's Industrial Areas Foundation, have conducted rent strikes and have won gains with regard to housing repair, etc. There is no evidence in Alinsky's TWO or any of his other projects that their gains are greater than those of comparable communities in Chicago or other cities. Again, there is a lack of hard data.

The limitations of Alinsky's model in Chicago are particularly outstanding because he has organized four different groups in this city and yet appears to have had no significant influence on the Daley machine—an avowed enemy.

[13] *Op. cit.;* Philip Hauser, "Conflict vs. Consensus," *Chicago Sun-Times,* December 13, 1964, Section II, pp. 1-3.

When antipoverty organizations produce as little as Alinsky's groups, they receive no end of criticism. But the Alinsky façade continues to enchant the press and thereby the public.

Alinsky constantly poses as anti-establishment, but the question is: which establishment is he opposed to? The organization of organizations that he produces in the local community often seems to become a new local establishment. He does not in any fundamental way challenge the city-wide or national establishments.

Perhaps more to the point, Alinsky's approach has not led to anything in the way of development, movement, national program, or national organization. It is possible to argue, of course, that some other group may come along and organize those people who have been aroused by Alinsky's organizers; but this does not seem to have occurred, an interesting fact in itself. Perhaps the Alinsky model fundamentally diverts people from the idea of larger organization. In his opposition to large programs, broad goals, and ideology, Alinsky diverts and confuses even the small masses that are included in his organization. This is most evident in the groups he has organized over the last thirty years; but even in TWO, his most positive example, there does not seem to be any significant movement toward a larger program. Recently TWO has been moving toward job training and psychiatry for the poor.

Alinsky's great concern that the people in the local neighborhood should develop their own goals by themselves leads further to the possibility of a localist agenda, because it is the organizer-strategist-intellectual who should provide the connections, the larger view that will lead to the development of a movement. This is not to suggest that the larger view should be imposed upon the local group; yet it certainly should be developed, in part, by nationally oriented leadership. It still can then be vetoed, amended, or accepted by the local population.

Many people who are not major supporters of Alinsky believe that he plays a valuable role in aiding less "radical" groups in the society to make more extreme demands. The argument goes: if a group makes powerful, extreme demands, the establishment is more likely to accede to the milder demands of liberals and other less militant forces. There is no question that sometimes this argument holds true, but it requires a careful analysis of the conditions under which it does or does not. Some years ago the militant posture and activity of Mobilization for Youth so highly sensitized the local governmental systems that any attempts by public-sponsored agencies to become involved in social action were thereafter looked at askance. Some people mistakenly believe that the violence and the riots in various ghetto areas have led to new programs related to these areas. But there is no evidence for this. What happens is that money will be spent for riot control and temporary programs to keep youngsters off the streets. Typically the money is taken from one program and simply transferred to another. There is no evidence of any expanded programming in relation to riots that have occurred, other than perhaps permitting the turning on of hydrants in hot weather.

It is not possible to offer here a full analysis of the conditions under which a more extreme movement makes it easier for a less extreme movement to achieve gains. Suffice it to say, however, that the extreme movement should probably possess genuine power which is more than locally based and should be able to have some relationship, short of complete disparagement, with the less militant groups. The civil rights movement in its earlier phase was illustrative. At that time, when the more militant groups such as CORE and SNCC were able to have an influence on the other civil rights groups and frequently coalesced with them, the movement had much greater influence as a whole.

The question has to be asked repeatedly, and not only as to whether an opposite effect occurs in response to an extreme demand, but also whether the goals would be achieved, independent of this type of demand. We must always ask, "What are the alternatives if the Alinsky position were not offered?" "How is Alinsky distracting and diverting from more significant programs of social change?" "Does he politicize the area, or does he simply direct people into a kind of dead-end local activism?"[14]

[14] See Paul Feldman, "The Pathos of Black Power," *Dissent*, January-February 1967, pp. 69-80.

RADICAL RHETORIC
VERSUS RADICAL GOALS

In some cases Alinsky probably does break a local stalemate and provides a door opener where nothing has been happening. The existing political power structure in Rochester, for example, responded to the coming of Alinsky by making counterpromises, etc. Frequently, however, as much energy is directed into exposing Alinsky, and little real change takes place. This, of course, is not a necessary condition, but it seems to happen frequently, probably largely because Alinsky is concerned with developing counterorganization rather than large-scale political change; his tactics, therefore, are in this direction and there is an underemphasis on methods of influencing the local power groups that cannot be directly attributed to the power of the Alinsky organization.

It is difficult to understand why Alinsky should be accepted as a radical by people knowledgeable about radicalism, since he has no basic critical analysis of American society, no program for large-scale institutional changes, and no national program whatsoever.

(The titles of Alinsky's books are most revealing with regard to the man who calls himself a "professional radical." He published *Reveille for Radicals* in 1945, and for some time he has talked about a book to be published called *Rules for Revolution*.)

Alinsky has developed no organization outside of local areas, and he eschews ideology, which he equates with dogma; he has no plan to assist the poor to become nonpoor and to leave poverty. He has never developed any national coalition with other major forces. Groups he has organized sometimes actually develop reactionary orientations (for example, the anti-Negro orientation of the Back of the Yards group in Chicago) . He provides no analysis of new developments taking place in the society that might have relevance for a long-range strategy.

The Alinsky formula assumes some kind of bootstrap magic by which individual neighborhoods can solve their problems through an almost Mao-like belief in the magic or efficacy of unaided human will. It seems doubtful in the extreme whether local communities can make up for an inadequate national growth rate, and, in many if not most cases, the local economy is a reflection of factors beyond its individual control. The Alinsky model may thus lead to profound conservatism in practice in which radical slogans and rent strikes serve as a substitute for coordinated programmatic national action. Neighborhood organization without adequate theory may produce no more than piecemeal noble gestures.[15]

Essentially, then, it is clear that what is radical about Alinsky's approach is its rhetoric—its emphasis on militant posture, and its anti-establishment mystique. Why, then, does such an approach appeal to many American progressives and radicals?[16] There seem to be at least three reasons:

(1)   There is a powerful underdog, anti-establishment tradition in America which can easily be transformed into a mystique of the poor in which there is little careful understanding of what significant, progressive roles an underclass can play in a national movement, if united with other forces, such as intellectuals and strategists. European history is replete with leaders who knew how to unite intellectuals and the underclass. American intellectuals are not especially politically sophisticated. They have few ideological traditions and little experience with the development of national political movements. Strachey, Laski, Bernstein, Lenin, Marx, and countless others developed strategy, tactics, ideology, and program. But Alinsky has only glamorous tactics, and *ultimately tactics without strategy become bad tactics.*

(2)   There is a bias in America for a kind of mindless, anarchic, pragmatic action, and a leader who ruthlessly calls for "getting things done," not talking a lot of bull, may have considerable appeal.

[15] From "Politics of Social Welfare." Paper prepared by Morton Long for Columbia University Conference, November 1965.

[16] This critique of American radicals who are influenced by Alinsky does not exclude myself. In an earlier article on Alinsky, though highly critical and never presuming him to be radical, I was to some extent taken in by magazine claims regarding his effectiveness. More recent events, further information, and analysis have led to the present position which sees him as highly ineffective and diversionary. See Frank Riessman, "Self-Help Among the Poor: New Styles of Social Action," *Transaction,* Vol. 2, No. 6, September-October 1965, p. 32. Also, F. Riessman, "A Comparison of Two Social Action Approaches: Saul Alinsky and the New Student Left," *New York State Psychologist,* Vol. 18, No. 2, April 1966.

(3) Finally, progressives and intellectuals in our society, nostalgic for the 1930's, awakened by the civil rights movement of the 1960's, and impressed by the activism of the young Left, have been searching for models to complete their early, unfulfilled radicalism.

To do this successfully, however, we will have to reappraise the potential trends and possibilities of the 1960's. Through combining our goals with these trends, we will be able to shape new radical programs and strategies different from those of the 1930's.

Frankly, we believe that many of the groups concerned with a radical program in America are caught up in stale images and biases. Thus, many radicals today one-sidedly emphasize conflict and demonstration tactics with little realization of the need to develop these into broader political tactics; they overlook the important cleavages within the establishment and the significance of many subestablishments, they possess a simplistic, finite view of power, and underestimate the significance of the expanding public sector of the economy. There is also a failure to grasp the dialectics of leadership, and hence too many radical-minded leaders in community action simply follow the new trends of the ghetto rather than provide the leadership that would come from large vision, national understanding, and theory.

SOME CONTRIBUTIONS OF SAUL ALINSKY

Alinsky has drawn attention to the significance of the power variable and the importance of conflict in social change. Moreover, he has emphasized the role of citizen involvement, particularly at the local level. In this sense, he is the forerunner of the new emphasis on decentralization, local control, and consumer power. Alinsky's own emphasis indicates a specific agenda for each community, and he does not particularly stress the need for an underlying thread which would draw together the various communities in a nationally significant program or movement, although his most recent attempt to influence a major change in Kodak hiring practices does indicate new tactics and new approaches directed at a national large-scale emphasis.

Alinsky sees himself also as the forerunner of black power, and as the Rochester FIGHT illustration indicates, he has been willing to accept a segregated black movement oriented toward achieving power. The developing black movement in the United States, however, and the student movement, bring together the local agendas in a new way. This is partly due to the role of the communications media and the dramatic character of the local programs, and partly to the fact that basic black interests, needs and developing programs lie beneath *specific local demands* and thus provide a thread building toward a large-scale movement.

II

THE WELFARE
CRISIS STRATEGY

One of the most talked-about and controversial programs to emerge from the various antipoverty efforts and discussions is the Cloward-Piven "strategy to end poverty." As the authors describe it, this strategy "is based on the fact that a vast discrepancy exists between the benefits to which people are entitled under public welfare programs and the sums which they actually receive. It is widely known, for example, that nearly 8 million persons (half of them white) now subsist on welfare, but it is not generally known that for every person on the rolls at least one more probably meets existing criteria of eligibility but is not obtaining assistance.

"The discrepancy is not an accident stemming from bureaucratic inefficiency; rather, it is an integral feature of the welfare system which, if challenged, would precipitate a profound financial and political crisis. The force for that challenge, and the strategy we propose, is a massive drive to recruit the poor onto the welfare rolls.

"A series of welfare drives in large cities would, we believe, impel action on a new federal program to distribute income, eliminating the present public welfare system, alleviating the abject poverty which it perpetrates. Widespread campaigns to register the eligible poor for welfare aid, and to help existing recipients obtain their full benefits, would produce bureaucratic disruption in welfare agencies and fiscal disruption in local and state governments. The disruptions would generate severe political strains, and deepen existing divisions among elements in the big-city Democratic coalition: the remaining white middle class, the white working-class ethnic groups and the growing minority poor. To avoid a further weakening of that historical coalition, a national Democratic administration would be constrained to advance a federal solution to poverty that would override local welfare failures, local class and racial conflicts and local revenue dilemmas. By the internal disruption of local bureaucratic practices, by the furor over public welfare poverty, and by the collapse of current financial arrangements, powerful forces can be generated for many economic reforms at the national level."[1]

The ultimate objective of this strategy: to wipe out poverty by establishing a guaranteed annual income. A number of extremely positive dimensions characterize the tactics and strategy evolved by Cloward and Piven:

(1) The involvement of a small number of welfare clients concentrated in a particular city, for example, can have a striking and rapid impact.[2] Thus, in New York City, which has been the main locale for the operation of the strategy, 6,000 members of the City-wide Coordinating Committee of Welfare Client Groups obtained special allowances for clothing and household furnishings, etc., which in June of 1968 led to a tripling of the previous year's monthly expenditures. This led to the flat grant of $100 per year for all

---

[1] See Richard Cloward and Francis Piven, "A Strategy to End Poverty," *The Nation,* May 2, 1966.

[2] In an article in *Transaction* in 1965, I postulated the positive value of a welfare rights movement. See *Transaction,* "Self-Help Among the Poor," September-October 1965, Vol. 2, No. 6.

families on welfare in New York City. It is clear that in order to be effective, this strategy does not need to involve large numbers of welfare recipients.

(2) The fact that the welfare rights movement relates to the large-scale demand for consumer involvement is another factor in its favor, drawing widespread support, the attention of the communications media and allies from the professional and intellectual worlds.

(3) The connecting of welfare rights to guaranteed annual income, which is a basic large-scale demand of many progressive forces in the society, is another positive attribute of this strategy.

(4) The strategy combines not only demonstrations and the organization of welfare-rights clients, but also tests the welfare laws in various ways, through hearings, court cases, etc.

(5) The movement, unlike the Alinsky approach, is nationally directed and has a clear program, goals, strategy and ideology.

In addition, some specific facts related to the New York scene have worked to great advantage of the movement. Thus the antipoverty commissioner, Mitchell Ginsburg, and Welfare Commissioner Jack Goldberg are highly progressive administrators who are particularly responsive to the needs and demands of welfare clients. Moreover, the Medicaid campaign led to the discovery of many people who were entitled to receive welfare payments and thus the welfare roles were swelled in New York State. This inadvertently dovetailed with the Cloward-Piven strategy by leading to a considerable increase in the number of welfare clients, thus further pressuring the New York State system. This in turn resulted in increased responsiveness and the providing of flat grants for clothing, etc., and even consideration of a total flat grant which in some ways is like a guaranteed annual income.

However, there are some limits of the Cloward-Piven strategy:

(1) Despite the fact that a large number of welfare clients throughout the country indicate a desire for jobs, the movement has only been slightly concerned with a job-creation demand as part of its program. It would almost seem as though the movement felt that its constituency might be lost if the welfare recipients obtained employment.

(2) It would also appear a mistake to de-emphasize the role of jobs because, as the Gallup poll of June 16, 1968, indicates, the public opposes guaranteed minimum income but strongly supports guaranteed work (78 percent favor a guaranteed work plan while 18 percent oppose it.)

(3) The fact that the movement is highly centered in New York City, which has many progressive traditions and progressive administrators, leads to something of an exaggeration of its effectiveness. However, if the pattern spreads to other cities, this limitation can be seen as simply part of a staging strategy where the most advantageous place is selected for the first round.

(4) In judging the effectiveness of any movement, the backlash that it produces must also be evaluated. The recent social security amendments passed by Congress, which attempt to force welfare recipients to work, provide an important illustration of the developing backlash in this area.

(5) There is another major difficulty in the argument, namely, that the proposal would actually end poverty in the United States. Since only one-fifth of the poor receive welfare, this is improbable. A program directed toward ending poverty must also be concerned with the millions of workers who receive less than the minimum wage, the subemployed and the unemployed. In other words, the Cloward-Piven program is an auxiliary program, not a central strategy.

(6) Many people like Cloward and Piven want to believe that a guaranteed annual income program would cost only $11 or $12 billion, but estimates by Lampman, Rein, and others indicate that the total cost in lost income from the people who might stop working, etc., may lead to a cost as high as $30 billion.[3] By contrast, with $30 billion we could create jobs for 6 million families or 24 to 30 million people. The vast institutional changes that would be produced in the society by this type of program are almost inconceivable. They go far beyond what would be involved in providing an income for 6 million families.

The Cloward-Piven strategy is limited by failure to grasp the long-term new economic trend of the society and its reflection in significant, developing strata. This is the trend toward

[3] See "The Guaranteed Annual Income," *American Child*, Summer 1966.

service work, particularly in the human services. The professional and the rapidly growing nonprofessional work force perform this work. They will be discussed more fully in Chapter III on New Careers.

A more embracing movement might be developed around a program directed toward widespread institutional changes with many pluses. Such a program could propose, for example, one million nonprofessional careers in the public sector. This kind of employment might be quite appealing to many people, not just welfare recipients. Moreover, when the nonprofessionals then become employed, they might be organized together with professionals in a national New Careers movement. Such a movement could have a wide impact on the professional systems, welfare colonialism, Negro-white unity, etc.

The nonprofessional group would probably include many young, potentially active, developing leaders and thus it is more likely that after the movement has begun, its own leaders will take over and provide their own momentum.

The guaranteed annual income is an important subsidiary goal in a social movement which must be built on permanent careers which, in turn, must lead to basic structural changes in the society and must be propelled by economically progressive groups that provide their own steam and funds. There is a great danger that the GAI appeal will be made central and thus divert attention from a much more decisive agenda. Essentially, any guaranteed-income program independent of job and career development for poor people is likely to be quite limited and would not furnish any basic cure for poverty. It does not provide a way of breaking the cycle of poverty.

III

NEW CAREERS

Basically, New Careers is a strategy to help the poor, underemployed as well as unemployed, escape from poverty.[1] It calls for a revolutionary reorganization of professional practices that would involve a complete change in approach to education, training, and manpower development. The most fruitful areas for setting up this program are in the schools (125,000 school aides have been employed through the Elementary and Secondary Education Act, Title I), hospitals, welfare agencies, institutions for mental health and community development and recreation—the so-called human-service occupations in the public sector. But some private industries are also exploring the possibilities the New Careers idea offers as a means of creating needed manpower and bringing the hard-core poor into the system.

[1] See Arthur Pearl and Frank Riessman, *New Careers for the Poor*, New York, Free Press, 1965.

The New Careers model proposes:

(1) That work can be restructured so that unskilled persons with minimum prejob training can very quickly perform useful functions at entry-level positions such as teacher aides, family-planning aides, community aides, health aides, probation aides, counseling aides, case aides, research aides, recreation aides, child-care aides;

(2) That while on the job, these aides can acquire further training during a portion of the working day, and can also obtain higher education, including college courses, at the work site in time released for advanced training;

(3) That this education can enable the aide to move up a career ladder, where he can function on increasingly higher levels of skill and responsibility and,

(4) That his job experience, on-the-job training, and site-based education can be combined with evening and summer college courses so that he can acquire a college degree in a relatively short period of time, and not be required either to leave his job to attend school full time, or go through the arduous process of attending college for many years at night while working full time during the day.

Overall the theory provides the opening for the development of a number of new occupational functions for both nonprofessionals and professionals.

For the professional it increases the possibility that he can play an enlarged role in program planning, consultation, administration, training, and supervision. The nonprofessional, on the other hand, not only performs the simpler tasks that do not require advanced professional skill, but in the human services he can also perform significant new functions that generally should not be performed by professionals, although they could in fact perform them. These new functions relate to the potential of the nonprofessional to function as a peer and in a more subjective fashion. What is being utilized here is the nonprofessional's special role and his time: he has more time to spend on an evening visit, on a long tutoring session, on routine grading of papers, or in an informal social discussion. This role permits him more equality, nor does it impose the distance or objectivity, inevitable and valuable for the professional's job. Most importantly, it permits him the subjectivity of a neighbor or friend.

These elements are unique to the human services and provide the special value that the untrained entry person can deliver in the service system, thus broadening the type of intervention as well as releasing the professional to do more advanced tasks. This reorganization of the human-service fields allows for a great increase in the quantity and quality of service.

Elements of the New Careers program are appearing in a good deal of legislation passed by Congress, *e.g.*, the Public Health Service Act of 1967, Social Security Act of 1967, Title I of the Elementary and Secondary Education Act of 1967, the Education Professions Development Act of 1967, etc.; but the most direct expression of the New Careers design is to be found in the New Careers amendment (the 1966 Scheuer Amendment) to the Economic Opportunity Act, which has provided funding for the institution of New Careers development programs in public agencies in over 100 cities.

A COMPLEX SYSTEM

New Careers is not a simple program to implement.* The creation of entry jobs is the first step. Then training must be made available immediately and integrally connected to these entry positions, and a visible career ladder leading to higher positions provided. Furthermore, all steps in the career line must be connected. In other words, if a teacher's aide doesn't require a high school degree, it would be too big a jump to the step of teacher, which requires a college diploma. Intermediate steps must be developed: assistant teacher, associate teacher, and so on, each requiring different amounts of education, training, and field experience. Training for these higher posi-

* Instituting New Careers is a complicated matter both technically and administratively in terms of the required interinstitutional negotiation and change. Not only must agencies accept the idea of employing untrained workers, but they must develop new job descriptions, a career ladder, some modification of their own training capability; in addition, educational and training components must be made available by educational institutions; personnel and civil service requirements must be modified, supportive services provided, new curricula prepared, and union and professional associations involved. All this is highly complex, including both technical and strategic dimensions. Moreover, all of this occurs within a governmental context in which there are Congressional and agency pressures and a limited number of middle- and top-level cadres to help plan and deliver the program.

tions has to be directly available through the job, and portions of the training provided in time off during the working day.

The idea is to provide people with employment first and diplomas later. This is directly at variance with one of the most popular concepts in America, namely, that an individual has to complete long years of education after high school before being allowed to perform a meaningful job. The system of formal schooling (in some professions up to ten full years) has automatically shut out a good many poor people. The New Careers approach will make it possible to achieve the relevant learning and more meaningful credentials in less time, while working at a job that pays enough to support a family. This can be done by setting aside eight hours of the working week for training and education, including college courses.

These courses should be carefully structured so that the relationship between theory and practical experience can be clearly grasped. Such an approach is particularly important for persons who have had negative education experiences and require a transitional stage to assist them back into the academic mainstream.

In a sense what is being proposed is an *Antioch for every man*. The advanced educational programs developed at Antioch, Bard, Bennington, and many other progressive colleges, requiring students to work for a portion of the year in the field and to relate this work experience to college courses, is an excellent model for connecting inductive (experience-based) and deductive (academic) learning. There is no reason why the model cannot simply be reversed so that the field experience and site-based training are the initial input, with the systematic college training being added to it or obtained concomitantly.

The special merit of the New Careers model is that it will immediately provide needed personnel in the human-service industries while the worker is acquiring the necessary education to move up the career ladder, if he so desires, and will also create a new source of recruitment of advanced manpower (*e.g.*, teachers) so urgently needed by our service economy.

It is still too soon to say how many will be able to reach true professional status. There are a few programs under way, however. New York City's Board of Education in February

1968 put into effect a four-step career plan giving 1,182 "residents of disadvantaged communities the opportunity to develop into teachers." This program, sponsored by the antipoverty agency, the Human Resources Administration, along with the Board, called for teacher aides and educational assistants in kindergartens, who would, through higher education and job-related courses taught by the City University of New York, be able to advance to higher positions. Similar career plans are being developed in a number of other cities.

The University of Minnesota in 1968 has developed such a plan, similar to others being tried in different parts of the country. Twenty hours of job time are set aside for aides to take courses toward a college degree or high school equivalency. More than two hundred aides are enrolled, taking credits toward an Associate in Arts degree, which is transferable to the regular B.A. program. The university is working with its local colleges and schools to develop special curricula for aides in two career lines, education and social welfare.

The New York City Department of Social Services (née Welfare) introduced in the fall of 1967 another illustration of a New Careers design. To begin with, the agency created two new nonprofessional positions—case aide and assistant caseworker—and it was envisioned that these people would work in teams with the professional staffs at local welfare centers, taking over many of the simpler tasks, freeing the case workers to handle more difficult problems. Hopefully these trainees, who were often members of the client community, would also improve communication with people in the neighborhood and add a new dimension to the quality of the service. In point of fact, the work of the entire department might be restructured to see who could do what meaningfully.

The program includes a half-day of supervised work experience, and a half-day of literacy training, general education, and counseling. The latter half-day is supervised by the City University as part of a design that includes up to 12 credits a semester of college courses. It is important to remember that job training alone doesn't guarantee anyone a career. There must be enough systematic learning to enable people to perform higher levels of work and to pass competitive tests.

THE MULTIPLIER EFFECT

The New Careers approach has a greater likelihood of being effective as an antipoverty strategy because it does not simply deal with income deficiency. Many poverty-related problems, bitterness, and frustration, derive not merely from income deficiency, but from lack of a meaningful life—which is closely related to having a meaningful job. Such a job will have the greatest multiplier effect on changing a variety of poverty-related characteristics that keep families in the poverty cycle. People develop their identity, their interest in life, through working and the organized relationship with others that work brings.[2]

In essence the New Careers strategy is directed mainly at providing significant opportunity to large numbers of poor people, enabling them to leave poverty. As a result of this goal, its deepest concern is in the area of permanent job status with the opportunity of moving toward professional and administrative positions. Together with this new status comes increased income, more services available, increased self-respect, greater power, and a lessening of alienation and anomie. The goal of New Careers is ultimately to produce enough jobs for the people who want them, and it looks to an expanding society in which more and more workers will be involved in technical, administrative, and professional activities and smaller proportions of the work force (perhaps for short periods of their lifetime, such as their youth) in productive, mainly automated, labor.

Furthermore, these expanded opportunities for the poor will not be at the expense of others. There is no assumption of a zero sum game in which there are a limited number of pro-

[2] Warren Benis observes that the work of the future will not be characterized by the dull monotony of the factory, nor by the bureaucracy of traditional large-scale organization. "People will be more intellectually committed to their jobs and will probably require more involvement, participation, and autonomy in their work." Warren Benis, "Beyond Bureaucracy," *Transaction*, Vol. 2, No. 5, July-August 1965, pp. 34-35. Benis believes that the leisure-centered society envisioned by Robert Theobald and other guaranteed-annual-income advocates may arise in the far distant future, but that long before that the new kind of work will become the "emotional creative sphere of life."

fessional jobs to be divided among the population. Rather, the assumption is based on a rapidly expanding professional market and new gradations within this market.

The New Careers position is directed at expanding the life chances of the poor. As the poor become part of the main-stream, important qualitative changes occur which cannot be measured by income alone. By moving from being unemployed —with no skills, opportunity, or education, lacking know-how, being wedded to a cycle of poverty, and having limited access to services and power—the poor person can become part of the job and career structure and reverse all this. Initially his in-come might only be slightly increased, but his total life situa-tion would be vastly different. Through becoming part of the career structure, he has the opportunity to acquire coping skills, has new access to services, education training, growth, power.

The New Careers design is applicable to people in all walks of life, in all classes, and at all levels. Part of the work aliena-tion that is so widespread in American society is related to the fact that even people who are not classified as poor do not have the option of starting and developing a new career after a certain age. Our system is full of dead-end jobs that people are locked into by an antiquated system of credentials. But nothing is more morale-destroying than an individual's know-ing that no matter how hard he works or how good his ability, he is literally stuck in a job that has no future.

This could be changed by introducing a system for trans-ferring academic credits and experience, so that an accountant, for example, might acquire a new degree in engineering with-out going through years of specialized training. An advanced professional should not have to go through the entire course program in order to become a doctor, if some of what he has learned is transferable.

Moreover, there are a large number of noncredentialed people in this society, including housewives, returned Peace Corpsmen, retired police officers, businessmen, college gradu-ates, and so on, who would be interested in developing a new career, if it could be done rapidly and on the job with ap-propriate salary.

The significance of the New Careers approach as an antipoverty strategy is based on the assumption that there must be a new Bill of Rights that includes the right to a permanent job, to a career, and to an income.*

Most discussions of the guaranteed annual income stress income free of work. While this is an important right, the priority should be guaranteed work, guaranteed annual wages. It should not be assumed that there are a great many people who cannot or will not want to work, or that meaningful jobs cannot be produced for them. Unemployability is related to the needs of the economy, as was illustrated during World War II when large numbers of supposedly unemployable people were rapidly recruited into the labor force and unemployment was reduced to about 1 percent of the civilian labor force. Today the combination of human-service jobs and automation allows for the possibility that large numbers of people—including the old, disabled, or untrained—can quickly be involved in entry-level human-service work. People who were hitherto believed to be unemployable can now be productively employed. Unemployability is related to the nature of work and how it is organized, not to the characteristics of people.

Most of the poor families receiving public assistance in the United States are either headed by people over sixty-five years of age or by women without husbands, and it is generally believed that these individuals are unable to work. This assumption is based on old concepts. In the new human-service jobs opening up in education, health, and welfare, many of these people will be able to find a place. The OEO Foster Grandparents' program, for instance, only touches the surface regarding what older citizens can do.* The development of child-care centers staffed by neighborhood workers will enable mothers to have their children cared for properly while they work; many of them will also work in the child-care centers.

Currently, some women who receive public assistance and

---

* It might be noted that other new rights which need to be emphasized today are rights to participation, legal rights, rights to various types of services, medical health education, etc. All of these rights are genuine possibilities in an affluent age, in a highly advanced economy where a small number of productive workers can produce all the basic goods required.

* OEO estimates that it employs over 130,000 nonprofessionals in its various programs, including Operation Headstart, which now has attached to it a New Careers-designed supplementary program for the career advancement of all its personnel.

were believed to be unemployable are showing considerable interest in acquiring jobs as casework aides in the New York City Careers Development program and in other similar New Careers programs in cities throughout the United States. The best way to develop a program for an antipoverty-oriented guaranteed annual income is to develop permanent jobs and careers, rather than stressing income independent of these jobs.

NEW CAREERS AND THE NEW ECONOMISM: JOBS VERSUS RIOTS

In order to win allies New Careers is going to have to go far beyond its job-creating role. Basically, the New Careers thrust is concerned with jobs. The accent on jobs has influenced the policies of a number of potential supporters, including the ADA (Americans for Democratic Action), the Urban Coalition, the Citizens Crusade Against Poverty, the AFL-CIO, the President's Automation Commission, the SCLC (Southern Christian Leadership Conference), and many other groups that view the development of large numbers of public-service jobs as the key to urban reconstruction and the reduction of ghetto unrest.

The job-oriented attack on poverty is a welcome relief from the earlier antipoverty emphases that stressed early-childhood education, training, and services as significant remedies.

But while New Careers can welcome the new stress on jobs it also recognizes that the job emphasis alone is a highly simplistic approach, albeit a good beginning point, to the major urban and metropolitan problems. Jobs alone will certainly not stop riots. We have only to look at the data presented by the Commission on Civil Disorders to see that nearly 80 percent of the "rioters" were employed; or the more recent data issued by the Labor Department which shows that the average income of 496 Negroes arrested in the Detroit riot exceeded $120 per week.[3]

The New Careers approach is very different from the simple job economism which is being widely advocated as a riot deterrent. First of all, New Careers is directed not simply at the unemployed poor, but at the employed poor who are major

[3] "The Detroit Riot: a Profile of 500 Prisoners," Department of Labor, March 1968.

participants in the disturbances in the ghetto. The New Careers approach does not merely seek to provide careerized jobs for the unemployed, but wants to *careerize the entire structure, thus upgrading all the employed workers*. Second, the New Careers approach from its inception has been concerned with the reorganization and improvement of human services which might provide an essential deterrent to the alienation which lies behind various forms of protest in our society, including ghetto upheavals.

Jobs alone will not produce the necessary reorganization of our society, nor the automatic improvement of our services, nor the reduction of the rampant new nihilism, anomie, disillusionment, and mindless anger that pervade large sections of the middle class and the disadvantaged segments of the population in different forms. Not even nonprofessional jobs in the human services will suffice. Nonprofessionals have long been employed, particularly in the hospital and health systems, with notably low morale, high turnover, and inadequate training.

This is not to say that it is not important that jobs be available. Holding a nurse's aide position even with minimal training may be better than being unemployed; being paid as a teacher's aide is probably better than part-time volunteering for PTA functions; and some useful work product is provided through employment, thus adding to the general pool of the society's resources. Furthermore, the increasing acceptance of the demand that the government provide jobs either directly or indirectly through training subsidies for private industry, also represents an important step forward, because it stresses the increasing importance of the public sector in our society.

Perhaps most important, the demand for jobs in the human services may be a first step toward much more decisive gains if united with other current demands for the accountability of human services, increased consumer involvement with regard to the character of these services, demands of professionals for the reorganization of these services, and increased allocation of resources for services instead of war-related products.

The thrust for jobs and careers must be transformed in these directions and allied with any other forces supporting such demands in a coalition that would include community groups, unions, welfare rights groups, professional associations, the liberal groups of the business community, and parts of the governmental establishments. With such an alliance, the job demand could be a new force that would provide programmatic dimension and direction. If, however, the demand for jobs is divorced from other issues in the reconstruction required in our society, it will have a limited positive effect and may even play a co-opting role.*

NEW CAREERS AND SOCIAL CHANGE

In any period of history there is typically a progressive underclass that is critical of the society, the methods of organization and control, and the central values. This was true of the working class in the 1930's and of the middle class earlier. These groups represented new, significant progressive economic forces and carried with them advanced demands for society. In the present period this is largely true of the Negro population. But this group lacks an economic base which would provide genuine power, resources, common interests, and everyday job-based interaction. These requirements could be provided for large numbers of people from the ghetto, working in human-service occupations, together with professionals who also have a strong interest in reorganizing these human services so that they, the professionals, can be productive and creative.* The New Careers approach allows not only for the development of a significant underclass, but may also stimulate a variety of institutional changes. It may be useful

* It should be noted that almost any positive social program can be transformed into its opposite through the manipulation of vested-interest groups. There are no perfect built-in guarantees. Socialism was transformed into National Socialism by the Nazis; the demand for community control, accountability, and decentralization can be transformed into anarchy, nihilism, and localistic diversion from national issues. Any national program must be viewed in terms of its dangers and constant vigilance must be maintained to avoid the dangerous consequences.

* Of course, this group of professionals does not represent the entire professional stratum. Some professionals are mainly status, guild, and credential centered. They have vested interests in maintaining irrelevant, outmoded technologies and attaching themselves to the monopolistic systems that protect these vested interests. Thus, it is not the entire professional stratum which represents a forward thrust, a progressive historical force, but an increasingly large segment—and this group may be allied with the nonprofessional human-service worker in a program directed toward a reorganization of the professional and the society.

to summarize briefly the potential institutional changes inherent in this program.

The New Careers approach has important implications for all types of training and college education. Certainly more training must be inductive and clinical. Thus doctors might be involved in field experience earlier in their training. (Western Reserve University Medical School has developed a plan along these lines.)

The New Careers concept proposes simultaneous education of nonprofessionals and their trainers. As this allows for a more rapid development of training capability, it has wide implications for the developing nations that mostly lack a training cadre. The New Careers concept may have special bearing on the development of population control on a wide scale in countries where the birth rate is preventing the rapid economic development of the nation—family-planning workers have been one of the most effective agents in persuading people to utilize the new birth control methods.

The New Careers concept holds out possibilities for people in all walks of life, and moreover offers significant hope to older people who are an increasingly high percentage of the population. That they need not start from the beginning to develop a new career is an extremely important option for them.

The New Careers concept has consequences not only for an increase in the quantity of services, but for linking and coordinating the human services. Nonprofessionals functioning as expediter-advocates in the new neighborhood service centers evolving all over the country can provide cement and energy in integration.*

The New Careers concept may also be a fundamental lever for institutional change. Because large numbers of nonprofessionals are likely to be employed in the educational system, there is the possibility of reorganizing educational practice;

* It is interesting to observe the effect of the New Careers trend on the older-type nonprofessionals who have long worked in settlement houses, hospitals, child care, etc. In New York City, for example, District Council 37 of the American Federation of State, County, and Municipal Employees of the AFL-CIO (which incidentally has in its union 20,000 hospital workers, and 7,000 school-lunch aides) has developed a plan whereby nurses' aides can become licensed practical nurses, with the required education and upgrading taking place on the job.

teachers will be freed for new roles and peer learning will be more fully utilized by nonprofessional teaching assistants. Hence the utilization of the new manpower is seen as a possible basis for bumping the system, unfreezing the equilibrium, and contributing toward a variety of social changes.

In some cases changes will be necessary for the New Careers idea to continue at all: changes in the civil service system and licensing requirements must be made to permit the employment of aides whose formal education has been limited; job-based courses must be offered by community colleges and universities if the nonprofessional is to develop a career line at all; new patterns of service including the nonprofessional in a meaningful, complementary team relationship to the professional must emerge; professional associations must adapt their practices and structures to include nonprofessionals.

Unfortunately, as Oscar Ornati points out, these changes have not been made.[4] In this first phase, at least, most of the nonprofessionals that have been employed are the "cream"; mostly they include those with higher education than the majority of poor people have. And while they appear to have worked effectively, they have not yet played a significant role in institutional or even agency change.

Not only have these changes failed to materialize, but also a number of problems have arisen, the solutions to which will require very careful planning. In some cases nonprofessionals have been glamorized as the leaders of the antipoverty war. In other cases they have been seen as a threat to professionals, and cleavages between professionals and nonprofessionals have arisen. Moreover, the New Careers model is interpreted by many professionals as a scheme whereby nonprofessionals go through steps on a career ladder to come out ultimately just like the professionals. Many professionals do not appear to understand the thrust to restructure the entire practice of both nonprofessionals and professionals in order to direct it toward producing a more relevant and meaningful service.

Some observers fail to see the significance of the *cross-sociali-zation* process whereby the professional is affected by, and can learn from, the nonprofessional as well as the opposite being

4 "Program Evaluation and the Definition of Poverty." Paper given at the Industrial Relations Research Association 19th annual winter meeting, December 29, 1966.

the case. Or, they see it as a smooth and simple process in which each teaches the other in a cooperative and pleasant team—most of the teaching going one way, from professional to nonprofessional. This is not the nature of significant change. The dialectics of change usually involve conflict, diversion, abrasiveness, and in general, an uneven flow—not a smooth, positive pattern. This change process is beginning to be experienced by professionals who work with nonprofessionals. They are discovering that the influx of large numbers of nonprofessionals is producing new demands, questions, pressures, styles, and patterns of work. Not all the new questions are constructive. The nonprofessional does not come into the system as the repository of all knowledge about the poor, nor does he raise only valuable questions that lead to adaptation of the professional system.

The point, however, is that despite some antiprofessionalism, the nonprofessional is an important source of pressure for change on both the service system and the professional. The exact direction of this change is not determined by the contribution of the nonprofessional, although his nonspecific effect is discernible. His general impact is in the raising of questions concerning the relevance of traditional practice and the organization of the service system—its rules, customs, traditions, pseudoprofessionalism, and ritual. If properly directed, this could lead to a much more authentic professional practice which is the goal of the New Careers program. For this to take place, however, a close and intensive interchange between the professional and nonprofessional is required; definite confrontations must be a basic mode of the training process. Specific, planned *co-training* of the nonprofessional and professional is a critical form in which the cross-socialization must occur and in which the special issues and problems can be raised.

Obviously this process cannot take place continually—it would be too abrasive and upsetting; some of the nonprofessional's training must occur with only nonprofessionals present, and similarly for the professionals. But an important aspect of the cross-socialization process must consist of joint training sessions, and trainers throughout the country must learn how to develop such discussions, control them, keep them to the point, but nevertheless bring out the real issues. This is an essential feature of a New Careers training design and it is vitally important if we are to avoid the professionals' discouraging the whole program because they want to keep nonprofessionals simply as helpers.

THE NEW CAREERS MOVEMENT

It is clear that institutional change does not automatically follow from the introduction of nonprofessional workers. What is most needed in the present phase is a New Careers movement. Of major importance is the need for nonprofessionals or New Careerists to be organized in order to express their desires for participation and social change, guarantee their security, prevent their manipulation, and finally to compel the necessary institutional changes in the civil service, educational, and other systems that will be necessary for New Careers to develop significantly.

The nonprofessionals must be united in a new type of organization.* This organization may well include elements of social movement, trade-union components, and some features that characterize professional associations such as the National Education Association or the National Association of Social Workers. Most important, a national New Careers movement must include not only nonprofessionals, but also professionals who favor the concept and want the human services reorganized.

At this moment a number of New Career organizations are being organized. Some include both professionals and nonprofessionals, while in other cases separate, parallel organizations are being formed, for professionals and for nonprofessionals, *e.g.,* The (New York) Citywide Paraprofessional Association. The leaflet stating the aims of the latter group is most revealing regarding potential demands of the New Careers movement.

The Citywide Paraprofessional Association Is—

—dedicated to careerizing paraprofessional positions

* It is probably going to be necessary for the nonprofessionals to belong to a number of different groups, to have, as it were, multiple memberships. Thus a teacher's aide might belong to a teachers' union along with professional teachers and also belong to a national New Careers movement which included professionals, nonprofessionals, and their friends.

—fulfilling the need to organize paraprofessionals into a special interest group regardless of union affiliation
—representative force for interpreting community demands
—an opportunity for paraprofessionals regardless of specialized fields to join forces around common concerns such as:

—job mobility
—accreditation for training and education by universities
—career development
—transferability of skills
—meaningful job descriptions
—freedom to criticize community services

—a vehicle for channeling community grievances
—a lobby for expanding existing legislation pertaining to paraprofessionals such as the:
1967 amendments of the Economic Opportunity Act, which provide for adult work training and employment programs;
1966 amendments of the Economic Opportunity Act (Scheuer Amendments), which provide for community employment and training programs to secure entry-level jobs and the *opportunity for continued advancement and careers.*
—a clearing house for information regarding training, education, and job opportunities

On June 19, at 7 A.M.—as Solidarity Day was starting for 50,000 other poor people in Washington—more than sixty psychiatric aides and other "serfs of the Kansas mental hospital system" moved quietly into eight wards of the Topeka State Hospital and took "administrative and clinical control."

Instead of withholding their labor by going on strike, the workers put on a "Hospital Improvement Action" under the slogan "We Care!" For twelve hours psychiatric aides—among the most highly skilled workers in the hospital system—created their model of how a hospital ward should be run.

Because they claim their work load is being increased to the neglect of patients, the aides put extra workers in each ward. Where one aide had serviced twenty to sixty-seven in a ward, they now brought in from four to ten workers into a ward. For the first time many patients were fed promptly, bathed quickly, and moved out into activities. When a patient got upset, instead of being forced into "Seclusion" because no one had time for him, "the aide sat down with the patient, found out what was bothering him, and did something specific about it," said one of the Improvers. Signs were posted: "This is a Union Administered Ward." Leaflets were handed out. Doctors, psychologists, nurses and other professionals continued to function in their clinical roles.

Thus began a most unusual union action: workers made the point that they were more concerned about proper patient care than were the Kansas authorities. In the weeks since the Improvement Action, they have proved to the community that patient care must begin with proper working conditions for the psychiatric aides and other nonprofessionals. The example of the Topeka Hospital Improvement Action initiated a precedent-setting strategy for workers in the field of human services. It highlighted the excruciating role of the nonprofessional; often, as with the psychiatric aides, he does professional work for the lowest pay. He is the key service worker; the condition of the service depends upon upgrading the job and providing him with training, a career ladder, higher pay and better working conditions.

These excerpts from Alex Efthims' *Nation* article, " 'We Care' in Kansas: The Nonprofessional Revolt" (August 5, 1968), point to dramatic new trends in the human services—the organizing of the workers of human-service agencies not only for "bread and butter" demands, but for the improvement of the quality of those services, the linkage of these new demands with the participatory demands of civil rights and community power forces in contemporary society. Unique in the activities of the Topeka aides, and common to New Careerists in general, is the concern for multiple benefits—not of the aides versus someone else, but of the aides for better service, closer community ties, new avenues to advancement; indeed, the slogan "We Care" typifies this new effort.

There are now in excess of 300,000 persons working as paraprofessionals in various human-service agencies, with public schools, OEO, and health institutions as the largest employers. While estimates vary, it is clear that there are large numbers of present jobs available but unfilled (Congressman James Scheuer talks of some 500,000 presently needed paraprofessionals), and that human-service work is the great growth area of the American economy—up as much as 100 percent in the next decade according to the Labor Department's "Occupational Handbook."

The development of paraprofessional opportunities has not been without effort and conflict. For some there have been the questions of whether noncredentialed persons could hold other than menial positions. The traditional orderly and nurse's aide positions in the hospital are examples of these "old" paraprofessional jobs, dead-ended and without any sense that the holder played an important part in the therapeutic process. Others have been concerned with the response of the professionals to the introduction of these new workers, doubly-new when we recognize that the paraprofessionals are often minority group members while the professionals are predominantly white. Administrators have been concerned with questions of supervision, chains of command, organizational plans, and budgetary support. Until recent date there has been little organized concern from those most directly affected by these developments, the paraprofessionals themselves.

Major strides have been made in the organizing of human-service workers in the past year, however. Mass meetings have been held, for example, in Los Angeles, Newark, Detroit, and Washington, D.C., of persons employed in New Careers programs as well as those in other poverty programs. In Los Angeles, plans are underway to organize the more than 7,000 poverty-program workers there, while in New York City, a Citywide Paraprofessional Organization already exists with membership from nearly a score of agencies throughout the city. Growing out of the convening convention of the New Careers National Council, held in Detroit in June 1968, an Ad Hoc Committee to Form a National Association of New Careerists was organized. The committee has participants in some twenty-two cities, has selected officers, held several meetings, helped organize mass meetings in various cities, has a

group of professional advisors, and is ready to move into full
operation.

The nonprofessionals will probably concern themselves
with four interrelated concerns:

1. The concerns of its members regarding wages, training
   stipends, increments, as well as the special concerns of
   those employed as paraprofessionals in agencies funded
   with federal funds such as grant termination, eligibility for such fringe benefits as sick leave, vacations,
   seniority rights, etc. Special concerns of paraprofessionals relate to issues of status—Where does the
   teacher aide eat? In the teachers lunchroom or, as has
   happened, in a special section of the student area?

2. Opportunities for relevant training, education and
   upgrading within the particular agency where the
   paraprofessional works, as well as the development of
   methods for lateral and diagonal movement between
   agencies. Another set of concerns relates to issues
   around testing, civil service regulations, credentialing,
   credit for work experience and life experience, adequate job descriptions.

3. Relationships between the human-service agencies and
   the communities which they serve. The paraprofessionals, as persons coming from these communities
   who continue to be a part of them, are of course a
   bridge between the two and are often hired for that
   purpose; however, the nature and quality of the service
   which the agency renders is critical to the community,
   and the paraprofessional does not see himself as a
   neutral agent simply allowing himself to be the link
   between poor service and poor people. Not only the
   quality of service, but also the processes through which
   the agency goes in determining the service are concerns
   of the paraprofessional both in terms of the participation of the staff that delivers it and the community
   that is the recipient.

4. The need for workers in the human services to bring
   together their various perspectives and agency activities so that there be established a coordinated approach
   to human-service work. Thus, within the national
   association will be paraprofessionals from educational,
   health, social welfare agencies, forming, in effect, an

industrial as opposed to a craft approach to organization.

The connection between this organization of paraprofessionals and present union groups is critical. Some of the activities of this group are similar to those of unions, but we do not believe that they are necessarily antagonistic. While the first of the concerns described above is closely akin to union-type activities, the others, especially items three and four, go far beyond union activities. I envision many New Careerists, as is currently the case, being members of unions in addition to their participation in this association. This is not significantly different from the multiple memberships of various professionals.

PART

II

IV

THE MOYNIHAN REPORT
AND THE
COMPENSATORY APPROACH

M any strategies for helping the disadvantaged are based on misconceptions. The Moynihan Report, for example, used the supposed inadequacies of the Negro family as an explanatory tool for understanding why the Negro has not taken his place fully in the economic structure of our society. Presumed family pathology, particularly illegitimacy, is held to be an important cause for the underemployment and inadequate education of the Negro.

The basic defect in the Moynihan thesis is a one-sided presentation of the consequences of segregation and discrimination. That damage has been done to the Negro as a result of discrimination cannot and should not be denied. But the

Negro has responded to his oppressive conditions by many powerful coping endeavors. He has developed many ways of fighting the system, protecting himself, providing self-help and even joy. One of the most significant forms of his adaptation has been the extended, female-based family.

To overlook this adaptation and instead to emphasize one-sidedly the limiting aspects and presumed pathology of this family is to do the Negro a deep injustice. And it is most inappropriate to attempt to involve people in change by emphasizing some alleged weakness in their make-up. People are much more readily moved through an emphasis on their strengths, their positives, their coping abilities. Thus Dr. John Spiegel, in providing psychotherapy for low-income populations, is most concerned to work with extended family rather than ignore it or stress its difficulties.

In the field of education there is a widely heralded, although essentially unsuccessful approach, which, like Moynihan's, one-sidedly attempts to develop a theory of action based on deficits. This is the "compensatory education" thesis.[1] It does not build on the action style, the cooperative (team) learning potential, or the hip language of the poor. Instead, compensatory education stresses deficits and attempts to build an entire program on overcoming these deficits.* Like the Moynihan family approach, it is one-sided in principle and doomed to failure in practice.

As long ago as 1955, I reported that Negro families in large numbers stated that education was what *they had missed most in life and what they would like their children to have.* These

[1] For a fuller critique of the compensatory theory, see Mario Fantini and Gerald Weinstein, *The Disadvantaged; Challenge to Education,* New York, Harper & Row, 1968.

* One should be very careful to specify what the presumed deficits are. It is not correct to talk about language deficiency as a general defect among low-income populations. It is more accurate to speak about deficiency in syntax and formal language. But in other aspects of language, such as the use of metaphor, rich adjectives, hip language, the connection between verbal and nonverbal communication, there is positive strength. A much more significant deficit of low-income populations is lack of school know-how and lack of system know-how. Similarly, in relation to the family, it is very important to specify what the supposed weaknesses are, and how these supposed weaknesses are translated into preventing the individual from functioning in the employment and education structures. The mechanism of this connection is often vague.

matriarchal Negro families are very pro-education, although they have long criticized IQ tests, all-white readers, condescending PTA's, and together with their children have indicated a strong desire for a livelier, more vital school. Their surprisingly tough, masculine youngsters would like a more male-oriented school. This can be achieved by hiring large numbers of males as nonprofessional teacher aides, recreation aides, parent-education coordinators. Since much of the learning in the family comes less from the parents and more from the brothers and sisters and friends on the street, this method of peer learning might well be adapted in the school itself. (Lippitt has demonstrated how disadvantaged sixth-grade youngsters helped fourth-grade youngsters for a short time during the week and both groups dramatically improved in their performance!)

If one wants to improve the educability of the Negro, it would seem much more relevant to stress changes in school practice and to develop this practice so that it is more attuned to the style and strengths of the population in question, rather than to emphasize the reorganization of the family. The latter emphasis seems much more indirect and less likely to produce the desired result. Similarly in the employment area, it would appear more appropriate to develop meaningful jobs for large numbers of low-income Negroes—e.g., nonprofessional jobs, where the job is provided first and the training built in, rather than being concerned about the family. In the Howard University Community Apprentice Experiment, it was demonstrated that highly delinquent, functionally illiterate Negro youngsters were able to function in nonprofessional jobs when the training was built into the job. Their life patterns and work patterns were markedly changed as a result of this new nonprofessional job experience even though there were no changes in their family pattern.

The emphasis on the deficits and damages of the Negro people kept sociologists from predicting the powerful Negro upheaval that developed into the civil rights movement. This behavior could not be accounted for by an emphasis on the weaknesses, deficiencies, and supposed lack of bootstraps. The uprising evolved from the Negro's *strength*, his protest, his anger, and when the conditions were ripe, these traits produced a powerful movement.

In response to the deficiencies of the system, the Negro has developed his own informal system and traditions in order to cope and survive. Storefront churches, the extended family, the use of the street as a playground, the block party, the mutual help of siblings, the informal know-how and self-help of the neighborhood, the use of peer learning, hip language, the rent strike, and other forms of direct social action are just a few illustrations.

The community-action phase of the antipoverty program is attempting to build on these positive traditions; thus the use of neighborhood service-center storefronts and nonprofessional neighborhood helpers are strategic features of the new community-action program.

Only by calling upon these traditions can the Negro move into the mainstream of our society, and, not incidentally, can our society benefit enormously from incorporation of some of these traditions. It is the Negro who is basically challenging our educational system and producing the demand for changes in educational technology and organization that will be of benefit to everyone.

It is only through full recognition of strengths that the condescension of welfarism can be avoided. Because if the have-nots have nothing—no culture, no strength, no anger, no organization, no cooperativeness, no inventiveness, no vitality—if they are only depressed, apathetic, fatalistic, and pathological, then where is the force for their liberation to come from?

V

THE STRATEGY
OF STYLE

I n order to utilize the strengths of the disadvantaged youngster it is necessary to understand his learning style. A
crucial element in the development of the individual's
learning relates to a careful understanding of the idiosyncratic style elements in the learning process. Students of
learning have focused a good deal on rather abstract and
molecular concepts that have been derived from studies of
pigeons and rats by B. F. Skinner and Clark L. Hull. These
concepts of learning are useful, but what has been overlooked
is the possible value of a more holistic, molar dimension of
learning which operates on the phenomenal level, and which
we refer to as style.

AN ILLUSTRATIVE MODEL

One index of style relates to whether an individual learns
things most easily by reading or hearing, or whether he learns

by physically doing things. These examples are not to be conceived as separate from one another. There can be such combinations as a visual-physical learner who learns in a slow, one-track fashion. As a matter of fact this last pattern is quite characteristic of the disadvantaged child. He learns more slowly; he learns through the physical (that is, by doing things, touching things) ; he learns visually, and he functions in a one-track way in that he doesn't shift easily and is not highly flexible in his learning. This is, of course, an ideal statement—a model.

Other dimensions of style reveal different aspects. For example, some people like to work under pressure; they like a deadline and they like tests. (Low-income youngsters do not like such conditions.) Some people like to leave a lot of time for their work, enjoying a slow tempo. Some people like to think or even read while walking. Some people like to work in a cold room, some in a warm one. Some people like to work for long periods of time without a break; some people like to shift and take frequent breaks. Some people take a long time to warm up, whereas others get into their work very quickly. Some people like to have all of the facts in front of them before they can do any generalizing, and others prefer to have a few facts. Some people like "props," some people do not. Typically, people do not know their own style nearly well enough.

COGNITION VERSUS EMOTION

Guidance workers have focused far too much on the categories of emotion, motivation, and personality rather than on the cognitive categories of learning and thinking. There has been much too much emphasis on the emotional approach in attempting to understand why a child doesn't learn. Little careful analysis is given to how the child's learning might improve simply by concentrating on the way that he works and learns, rather than on his affective reasons for not learning. This thesis is almost directly counter to the current view. Today if a child doesn't learn (and if he has intellectual ability) , it is quickly assumed that his difficulties must be due to some emotional block or conflict. There may be a different way of looking at the problem. He may not be learning because his methods of learning are not suited to his style, and hence he cannot best utilize his power. Even where his troubles are in part emotional or due to conflict, it still may be possible to ignore this particular focus and concentrate profitably on the specific expression of the difficulty itself—his learning pattern. Even if one rejects the premise that the emotional causes have been overemphasized, one may still give a willing ear to the possibility of dealing with crucial problems of learning in nonemotional, nonpsychodynamic terms. Unfortunately, teachers too often have behaved like psychologists and social workers. It seems that they do not sufficiently stress learning processes and styles of learning, apparently preferring motivational categories. One way to build up appropriate prestige in the teaching profession is *not* simply to borrow from psychologists and sociologists, but to concentrate on the development of what education is most concerned with—learning and teaching. When one does borrow from psychology, it may be better to concentrate on learning and cognition rather than personality and motivation.

ANIMALS AND MEN

If we examine the outcome of teacher-education courses in learning, educational psychology, and the like, we are usually forced to the suspicion that they amount to very little. Borrowing heavily from animal-learning experiments (which by itself is not necessarily bad), such courses are victimized by the fact that the particular concepts and formulations developed in the animal literature have not been easily applicable to human learning problems—whether a child learns slowly, whether he is a physical learner, or whether it takes him a long time to warm up. Although these problems are nearer to our subjective experience, the psychological literature and animal experiments have not really helped us very much to deal effectively with them. When educational psychology courses have actually studied human learning, the focus has not been on the significant problems that are related to style. When they attempt, for example, to deal with study habits, they are entirely too general. There is a great deal more to study habits than meets the eye of the introductory psychology textbook. The typical suggestions in the chapter on study habits are based upon various experiments which seem to indicate that distributive learning is better, that one should survey material first, etc. But very little is directed toward the *idiosyncratic* factors that are involved.

For example, some people simply can't tolerate surveying a chapter first. They become so anxious, so disturbed, by being asked to look at the overall view of the chapter that they can't function. These people want very much to read a chapter atomistically. This is their style. It won't help simply to tell such a person that he is not proceeding in the right way and that he really ought to read the chapter as a whole first. The same is true in terms of the general recommendation that one should have a quiet place to study. Strangely enough, some people study quite well in a noisy place, or with certain kinds of noise, and completely quiet places are not best for them. Some people take a long time to warm up; consequently, a great deal of spacing (or distribution) of learning would not be useful for them. This is their style. But the textbook does not tell you this because, in general, spaced learning has proven to be most effective.

The same argument applies to examinations or tests. For some people a test provides just the right mild anxiety to stimulate the integration of a great deal of material that needs to be learned. On the other hand, there are large numbers of people for whom tests are terrible because they disorganize them, make them too anxious, and thus prevent them from working. Tests are not conducive to the style of these individuals. When others argue that tests are marvelous because they aid pupils by providing corrections and criticism, they are referring to persons with a different style. Undoubtedly, tests work well for some pupils, but there are others who forget their wrong answers on tests because it disturbs them so much to remember them.

There is a great deal of controversy in the traditional literature on the very question of whether repression of wrong answers occurs or whether "punishment" for giving the wrong answers on tests helps to produce better recall. I am suggesting that two different kinds of styles are involved here. For some people the information that they gave wrong answers is extremely useful and challenging. If this information is called to their attention in a positive and stimulating way, it makes the wrong answer the figure in the foreground. It draws the incorrect responses to their attention in a constructive manner. For other people, knowing that they have made a mistake is extremely disturbing, destructive of their morale, and leads to a repressing of this material. Therefore, depending upon one's style and one's way of dealing with these problems, tests may or may not be useful.

STRATEGIES OF MODIFICATION

The task is to try to formulate the possible ways in which the strengths of the individual's style can be utilized and its weaknesses reduced or controlled.

Take as an example the "games" focus of low-income youngsters. They like to learn things through games rather than through tests. To put something in the form of games is an excellent transitional technique for winning their interest. A disadvantaged youngster who likes to learn by listening and speaking (aural style) is unlikely to change completely and become, say, a reader. This is not to suggest that such a pupil will not learn to read and write fluently, but his best learning, the long-lasting, deep learning that gets into his muscles, is more likely to derive from speaking and hearing.

In approaching the problem the first aim is to have the person become aware of the strengths and potentials in his style—because this is going to be the source of his power. Thus, if a disadvantaged individual has a physical style, he has to learn the special attributes of this style and how to use them. The guidance counselor or teacher will have to help him overcome the invidious interpretations of this style that are prevalent in our society.

Take an illustration of a different type. A low-income youngster tells us that he sits down to work but cannot concentrate. It is extremely important at this point (and this is crucial in the diagnosis of style) to ascertain as precisely as possible exactly what takes place in this youngster's routine. For example, when does he study? What time does he come home from school? What does he do first when he comes into the house? He may say:

I come home, throw down my books, and then I start to remember that I have to do some work. So I get out my books. I try to work. I take out the book, but my mind wanders. I look at the book; I look away. I can't get into the work, and after a few minutes of trying this, I begin to feel discouraged; I begin to feel bad. I feel I can't work. I'm no good. I get very worried, panic builds up, and then I run away from the work.

There are many possibilities operating in this pattern. One possibility is that this youngster has a slow warm-up period. He does not easily get into something new; he does not shift from whatever he's been doing before (whether he's been outside playing ball or inside listening to the radio). This may be due to a number of reasons. He may be a physical learner. If he is a physical learner, he must be involved physically in the work process. He has to get his muscles into it, and this takes time. If this is our student's pattern, then he must come to understand that although he is slow to warm up, this is not necessarily a negative quality; it is simply a different way of approaching work.

Actually it may very often be connected to perseverance, once he gets involved! Once he is immersed, he may go deeper and deeper and not be able to shift away from the work easily. The inability to shift doesn't then operate as a negative feature, but as a positive element in his style. But the youngster described here rarely gets to this point. It's not that he doesn't persevere somewhere, in baseball or somewhere else. But in his school work he's never gotten past the point of the slow warm-up. In order to use his pattern effectively, he has to schedule his time so that he works for one hour. That's no good because it takes him a half-hour to warm up. Even if he were to be successful and stick with it for the half-hour as a result of a teacher's or guidance worker's support and stimulation, the problem of having only a short time left to work would remain at the end of the half-hour. Consequently he has to plan a longer time period of work and recognize in advance that it will take him about a half-hour to warm up. In other words, the person who would help him must give him a definition of his work pattern in order to realize the positive potentialities in it.

STRENGTH OVER WEAKNESS

When this new definition is provided, it is probable that a number of consequences will follow. Over a period of time the warm-up period will shorten because part of the difficulty in the long warm-up is the anxiety that emerges as an individual tries to get into the work and fails. Thus, by getting into the work, his anxiety decreases, and his interest has a chance, concomitantly, to increase.

To take another example, one in which the person's strengths can be used to deal with his weaknesses. How do you teach a person how to read when reading is not his basic style? Everyone is going to need reading ability and writing ability regardless of his style. In order to teach reading to youngsters for whom it is stylistically uncongenial, one may want to use role-playing, which is more related to the physical style of the individual. He can read about something that he just role-played, or he can read about a trip he has recently taken. While teaching reading under these conditions, the teacher must remember that he is not developing a reading style; he is developing a skill, a *balance* in the pupil's style. He is developing minimal efficiency in an area which is not rooted in the learner's style. In a sense the teacher is going after his Achilles heel—his weakness, the reading difficulty—by developing it through his strength, whether it be visual, physical, or whatever. This is a basic tactic for defeating or limiting the weakness by connecting it and subjecting it to the strengths.

MINIMAL GOALS

There are some other things one can do in employing the strategy of style. Various transitional techniques can be used, for example, in overcoming some of a pupil's educational weaknesses. Illustratively, low-income youngsters come to the school situation ordinarily with a very poor auditory set. They're not accustomed to listening to people read stories to them. This kind of pattern can be limited quite a bit and can be overcome up to a point. I don't think that the school can develop a basic aural style in such children, but effective teachers can teach them to learn through listening even though this isn't their *best* mode of learning. One technique was developed by a man who worked with schizophrenic children. The technique was simply to make a game out of the auditory problem. He would ask, for example, What is six and five? Everybody in the class would have to answer several times. The pupil cannot fall asleep in such a class. Answering once doesn't leave him free because he may be asked the same question (or somewhat different ones) often. This is an excellent technique for waking up youngsters, and it has been effective with low-income students who are not used to listening. The objective is to bring them up to minimal listening ability, up to grade level. Low-income youngsters can be brought far beyond grade level in most areas, because they have considerable creative ability; but in their areas of weakness, it would be good simply to bring them up to grade level. In areas of weakness our primary aim should be functioning on a minimal level of adequacy so that weaknesses will not destroy strengths. Techniques of the kind described may be useful in reversing habits and sets which have grown out of the negative aspects of the person's style.

To sum up: in everybody's style there are certain strengths, and each of us has his own Achilles heel. The issue in developing a significant change in a person is related to how one gets to the Achilles heel and how one utilizes the strengths. This is the central problem of the strategy of style, especially in its application to the low-income pupils of our urban schools.

VI

with Frank Alberts

DIGGING "THE MAN'S" LANGUAGE

In order to make contact with the style of the disadvantaged youngster, it may be necessary, first, to understand his language. Each of us has at least one second language he or she didn't learn at school. It may be the *lingua franca* of executive committees ("Let's finalize this."), of cocktail party analysts ("His trouble is, he's a latent heterosexual."), perhaps of *belles lettres* ("It was a Hemingway meal.").

Whatever its derivations, the second language is clearly understood by its educated middle-class users to function as an additive to their primary language. And that primary language

—the customary English of our schools, more or less standard-ized in pronunciation—is one of the principal distinguishing marks by which the user is recognized and accepted into the middle class.

What happens, however, when one of those languages that the middle class regards as secondary—in this case, the dialect of the school-age child from one of our nation's disadvantaged urban areas—is discovered to be functioning as a primary language? More pertinent, how is a teacher charged with in-structing these children in standard English to perform her task with any degree of meaningfulness?

The answers to these questions, both of pivotal importance in any educational attempt to work with the poor, are exempli-fied in the following story about a teacher in a grade school in a disadvantaged area.

One day after class, as she was putting on her hat to leave for the day, one of her students approached her with the compliment, "That's sure a tough hat you got on."

The teacher, who had heard enough Hip spoken among her charges to be with it, tried the time-honored approach to cor-recting the boy: "Don't say 'tough.' Say 'pretty' or 'nice.' "

The boy thought about that a moment, then concluded: "Okay, but that pretty hat sure is tough."

That might have been the end of this particular story except that this particular teacher also gave some thought to the exchange.

First, she realized that she had come up against a case of linguistic inversion—a social situation in which a dialect was the primary language.

Second, and most important, the teacher recognized that by attempting to correct her student's speech in the conventional way, she had confused him about the nature of the avowed teaching objective. Worse, she had antagonized him. To the student's mind, the teacher had been asking him, not so much to learn something, but to reject something—his primary language, the slang, the nonstandard Hip spoken in his home, on his street, among his friends and neighbors. The result was hostility—a determination by the student to *not* learn—ex-pressed, with just the necessary touch of humor, in the put-down phrase, ". . . that pretty hat sure is tough."

In short, this teacher had hit on a truth fundamental to the fact of language: One's primary language, because it is pri-mary, is not to be denied lightly, for it is, in very basic ways, one's own self. Asking the disadvantaged child to suppress the language he brings to the learning situation is equivalent to demanding that he suppress his identity, and all the defenses that go with it—in Hip parlance, to require that the child "blow his own cool."

Cognizant of this truth, the teacher assayed a new approach to the business of teaching her students standard English. She made a game of it, the Dialect Game. Taking a term she had often heard her students use among themselves—the word "cool"—she asked them to explain its meaning in *their* lan-guage. After some understandable hesitation, she got the fol-lowing examples:

"Well, you know—like, you dig this cool sound."

"You play it cool."

"The fuzz falls by—you cool it." (Laughter)

Then the teacher asked her class how the same thing might be said in the language the students heard on TV or radio.

"Calm," "casual," "collected" were some of the answers she got, to which she added the more formal "nonchalant."

As the lesson proceeded, the students—who usually all but fell asleep during formal English classes—relaxed, their interest increased. They became aware that they were playing a game, digging the teacher's jive. They were picking up new words, new ways of expression in a context which did not demand that they reject their own language. In short, they were learn-ing standard English as they might learn a foreign language, a second language.

They were also learning about language itself, its forms and the social roles it plays. In their discussion of the word "cool," for example, they learned not only the denotative synonyms for the word in "The Man's" language, but also that standard English really possesses no perfect equivalent of "cool," no term with its rich connotative content.

The same is true, the students began to realize, of many of the Hip words and phrases that make up their primary lan-guage—"far out," "hang-up," "cop out," to cite a few. The stu-dents were becoming familiar with a basic fact of language—the concept of nuances, the age-old bane of translators. By being asked to approach standard English as if it were a foreign language, the students became aware of the essential untranslatability of much of language *per se.*

This in turn led to their understanding why words and phrases foreign to every primary language are incorporated in that language intact, without translation—for example, *coup d'état* and *leitmotiv.* In much the same way—and with far more psychological impact—the students learned that many of the Hip words and phrases that make up their primary language have been accepted for usage in standard English conversation. Knowing this, they were in a position to equip themselves with a basic sense of linguistic style, which can be simply defined as the ability to choose among words and phrases according to their social appropriateness.

The key ground rule of the Dialect Game—for both teacher and teaching situation—is acceptance of the students' nonstandard primary language. The instructor who makes clear to his pupils that their primary language is not something to be denied or suppressed, but is in fact a linguistic entrée to that other language which, in more formal circumstances, can produce more effective results, is building firmly on positive grounds. The importance of this teaching method in assisting the disadvantaged to gain entrance to our nation's Greater Society has nowhere been more dramatically stated than by Negro author Ralph Ellison, when he wrote:

> If you can show me how I can cling to that which is real to me, while teaching me a way into the larger society, then I will not only drop my defenses and my hostility, but I will sing your praises and I will help you to make the desert bear fruit.

There are a number of simple adaptations of the Dialect Game that fit a variety of special teaching situations. For example, one of the authors recently employed a "Hiptionary" in a completely systematic and formal way in tutoring a disadvantaged high school student in standard English. The "Hiptionary," or "Hip workbook" to be more accurate, was based in large part on the unpublished *The Other Language* developed by Anthony Romeo at Mobilization for Youth. Among the Hip words and phrases employed were:

bug   to disturb, bother, annoy
ace   best friend
fuzz   police

The rather immediate result of this approach was that the student—in this case, a teen-age girl—learned a great many standard English words for the Hip words with which she had long been familiar. She derived genuine pleasure from and pride in her growing facility to use "big words."

The important point about teaching standard English to disadvantaged students equipped linguistically with Hip or nonstandard dialects is that the process is additive—the teacher *builds on* what the pupil brings to the teaching situation; he does not *take away from* the pupil. In this way, the students' sense of language—all language—grows, and with that growth can come a love of language and its literary forms.

The implications of this positive, additive approach to the teaching of standard English is strikingly exemplified in the case of another disadvantaged group, the Puerto Ricans. The usual classroom approach in the United States is to require that these children speak only English, not their native Spanish, usually on the grounds that this is the best (with the implication that this is the *only*) way to learn standard English.

This may be a perfectly acceptable way of teaching a new language to an adult, but it plays psychological havoc with a child from a minority culture. In his mind, the teacher's insistence on "English only" is equated with "no Spanish here," an outright rejection of the culture associated with his home, family, and friends. One more rejection has been added to the many he has experienced in the society to which he has been transplanted.

The result is resentment, a dragging of the feet in matters linguistic—in no way alleviated by the fact that, while the other children in the class already know a good deal of standard English, the Puerto Rican is automatically in the inferior position of having to acquire that language.

THE OTHER LANGUAGE

The language of the streets is constantly changing, and it varies from place to place. Yet the choice of words often reveals a great deal about the attitude toward the thing or the activity that the word describes. The brief glossary below is taken from *The Other Language,* compiled by Anthony Romeo for Mobilization for Youth, 214 East Second Street, New York, N. Y.

ax	musical instrument, horn
bad	stylish, nice, in vogue
burn	to shoot, cook food, smoke marijuana
cop out	to avoid conflict by running away
crib	house, apartment, residence
diddy bop	member of a gang, usually a hostile or aggressive gang
fair one	to fight another person alone, neither opponent receiving help
far out	not comprehensible, not desirable, outlandish
gestaps	the police
gray boy	Caucasian
hang-ups	problems
lay up	relaxing
mink	girl friend
mother	salesman of illegal drugs
paddy	Caucasian
sky piece	hat, fedora, beret
splib	Negro
teach	male or female who bears a resemblance to school teacher because of the authority he or she may have, usually used in a derogatory sense
vacation	to be in jail

The Dialect Game can be varied for this situation too. Instead of emphasizing the need for Spanish-speaking children to learn English, the teacher can reverse the situation so that the Spanish-speakers teach their language to the English-speakers. The advantages are:

First—and perhaps, psychologically, foremost—the Puerto Rican children are placed temporarily in a position of some superiority, for they are helping their classmates. Second, both Spanish and English become important in the classroom—both are recognized as languages, and *as languages* both are acceptable. Third, the English-speaking students get an opportunity to learn a foreign language. And fourth, the Spanish-speaking children, in order to teach their language to an English-speaker, must acquire an increasing knowledge of English in order to communicate with their classmates.

Of course, the process is not that simple and requires additional techniques. But in the broader societal context this variation of the Dialect Game, because it employs the child's primary language as the basic element of his culture, eliminates the gratuitous condescension inherent in classroom concentration on superficials such as "colorful" native costumes and customs or "songs from many lands." The primary objective is to teach language, and this approach does. But one of its principal benefits is that it also teaches culture, and, more importantly, a respect for culture.

Once again, the process is additive and positive—and these qualities are essential if we of the middle class are to be taken seriously when we assert that we want to bring the strengths and interests of the deprived into the mainstream of American life today.

VII

with Lita Paniagua

A NEW EDUCATION STRATEGY

WHERE THE JOBS ARE

Victor Fuchs, the Associate Director of Research of the National Bureau of Economic Research, states that virtually all of the increase in employment from 48 million in 1947 to 72 million in 1967 has been in the service areas of the economy—hospitals, schools, social work—while employment in the production of goods has remained relatively stable. He calls ours the first service economy; that is, we are the first nation in which more than half of the employed are not involved in the production of tangible goods.

Moreover, jobs in government—federal, state, or local—will climb almost 4 million, or nearly 40 percent, during the next decade; jobs in mining will continue their long decline and the number of jobs in agriculture is slated to drop another 23 percent in the 1965-75 period; job opportunities in health will increase across the board, encompassing not only the physicians and nurses but also dentists, dental laboratory technicians, x-ray technicians, physical and occupational therapists, dietitians, and veterinarians.

Some 15,000 persons are needed to replace those leaving the field of social work and to staff new services. The total number of M.S.W. graduates from schools of social work throughout the nation is only 3,500 yearly. The HEW task force on Social Welfare Education and Manpower predicts a need for 100,000 social workers plus 50,000 additional workers for HEW agencies alone by 1970. The U.S. Department of Labor foresees a deficit of 500,000 elementary and secondary school teachers by 1970.[1]

The National Commission on Technology, Automation, and Economic Progress estimates a need for 5.3 million public service workers in the United States. A potential of 4.3 million jobs has been estimated by Greenleigh Associates, Inc.

The National Advisory Commission on Civil Disorders reports that nearly 80 percent of those involved in rebellions were employed in the intermittent low-status unskilled jobs to which ghetto residents are confined. The report states:

> Even more important perhaps than unemployment is the related problem of the undesirable nature of many jobs open to Negroes. Negro workers are concentrated in the lowest-skilled and lowest-paying occupations. These jobs often involve sub-standard wages, great instability and uncertainty of tenure, extremely low status in the eyes of both employer and employee, little or no chance for meaningful advancement, and unpleasant or exhausting duties. . . . The concentration of male Negro employment at

[1] "By 1975 there will be almost 20 per cent more persons of school age than there were in 1965; many more of this age group will be going to school, and an appreciable number of children will start school at an early age. Many others will stay in school longer, go on to college and aspire to higher degrees. Given possibly twice as many students and a reduction by a third of pupil-teacher ratios, it is probable that by 1975 over 5 million persons will be needed in teaching roles. It is absolutely impossible to develop such persons without some utilization of educational personnel other than certified teachers in the classroom." Arthur Pearl, "New Careers and the Manpower Crisis in Education," in Frank Riessman and Hermine Popper, *Up From Poverty*, New York, Harper & Row, 1968.

the lowest end of the occupational scale is greatly depressing the incomes of United States Negroes in general. In fact, this is the single most important source of poverty among Negroes. It is even more important than unemployment.

Kenneth Clark substantiates the importance of jobs that provide the worker with dignity, opportunity, and respect. He found a higher correlation between unskilled work and social pathology than between unemployment and social pathology. Clark says: "Apparently, the roots of pathology in Central Harlem lie not primarily in unemployment but in the low status of jobs held by the residents of the community."[2]

Forty-six percent of those served by vocational education programs in 1967 were in home economics or agriculture and only 4 percent and 1 percent, respectively, in technical occupations and health occupations, according to the Essex Commission Report. The Report goes on to state that "there is little evidence of much effort to develop programs in areas where critical manpower shortages exist."[3]

It is clear then that the vastly expanding areas of employment in the United States are likely to be the human-service industries—health, education and welfare, recreation, community development, and research. It is also evident that our schools have not been preparing youngsters for positions in these rapidly growing sectors of the economy; nor are out-of-school adults being prepared in sufficient numbers for these jobs on the inaccurate assumption that it is too late for them.

THE EDUCATION LOCKOUT

What are the ways in which a student today can prepare for a career in the human services? If he wants to become a teacher, a public health specialist or a social worker, he will typically follow one path: four years of academic curriculum in high school, followed by expensive and lengthy specialization in college and graduate school. The prospective teacher, for example, is not allowed to do practice teaching until he has completed years of courses, many of which are not relevant

[2] See *Youth in the Ghetto*, New York, Haryou, 1964.
[3] Report of the Advisory Council on Vocational Education (the Essex Commission), January 1968.

to his chosen field. This method not only consumes time and money, but also may well stifle enthusiasm.

Another path to a career in the human services is via the night-college route, which can take up to ten years of study. The dropout rate is high because most night-college students hold full-time jobs during the day, and it requires tremendous motivation and a high degree of self-discipline to stick to the program.

Furthermore, this academic route, whether undertaken in day or night college, is open only to those students judged to have "college potential" according to traditional standards. It is in effect discriminatory. (It also makes youngsters commit themselves as to whether or not they are "college bound," too early.) There may be thousands of other students with a high degree of talent for working with people, who, regardless of their interest in entering the human-service fields and their latent ability to do so, are now edged out of the road, and locked into old-line vocational courses leading only to humdrum wage earnings in jobs fast being eliminated by industry's sophisticated technology.

Vocational training of the type that has become traditional in the nation's public high schools is not programmed at present to prepare students for employment in the human services. Its orientation is toward agriculture and manual skills, although these sectors of the economy show a declining growth rate. Another drawback to this kind of vocational education is that it limits students to only one kind of work. Should the demand for a certain kind of skill disappear, or should a student desire to follow another line of work, the results of such narrow training can create extreme hardship. If a person who has followed a vocational course in high school wanted to go to college later on, he would have to spend much time making up courses before he could apply for admission.

On the prestige scale of a high school, vocational courses have low status; they connote failure, and this becomes increasingly true as the economy moves toward the production of services rather than goods.

There is hardly any high school education oriented toward preparing youngsters to be research aides, teacher aides, social work aides; nor has the high school in any way attached to these occupations a model providing work-study experience, which would not only introduce a highly valuable new way of developing trained workers, but also might be particularly appealing to large segments of the population hitherto screened out of these occupations. Even specially designed college programs, such as New York University's Project Apex, directed toward recruiting disadvantaged high school students, have not tailored their courses to prepare these youngsters for various landings in the human-services area; nor have they carefully combined accredited work experience and college courses. The junior colleges and community colleges too have been slow in preparing people for the human services. Moreover, the Associate in Arts degree is often terminal; that is, it does not articulate with or *allow the student* to go on to higher education and professional status.

Some positive efforts are being made of course. The government, the universities, and private foundations are investigating new ways of educating persons for employability, but these programs do not reflect an awareness of the burgeoning importance of the human services, with some notable exceptions:

> The Job Corps at Clearfield, Utah, has a six-month intensive on-the-job training program which prepares youngsters for entry-level positions as teacher, counselor, and recreation aides.
>
> Howard University, in conjunction with Cardozo High School in Washington, developed a work-study program wherein high school students were educated to become health aides, child care aides, etc.[4]

However, even in such instances as the above, one may ask whether the academic aspects of the programs are broad enough—that is, is there sufficient background given in general cultural subjects?

TOWARD AN INTEGRATED
VOCATIONAL ACADEMIC CURRICULUM

It might be appropriate at this time to reevaluate the practicality of vocational and academic education as they are

---

[4] See *New Careers Newsletter*, Vol. I, No. 2, August 1967.

now conceived and expand their meaning to include preparation for work in the human services. It would in fact seem
that all the old pathways to employability which have existed
for so long should be rerouted and redesigned to become a
speedy highway with ample room to transport many different
kinds of travelers, and with many turnoffs leading to a wide
variety of destinations.

It is necessary to create courses of study so concretely connected to employment upon graduation that students will be
highly motivated to remain in school. But at the same time
such courses should increase each person's capacity for making
a wide number of choices, so that at any point in his life he
may be ready and free to accept new opportunities that arise.
As Arthur Pearl has stated so well:

> Basic to any concept of freedom is the range of occupa-
> tional choice available to citizens. Evolutionary events
> have placed the school in a salient position in the matter
> of occupational choice. . . . unskilled labor is becoming
> obsolete and options for the poorly educated decline daily;
> and schools, rather than increasing options, lead to limited
> choice.[5]

One way to increase the number of career options for high
school students would be through a reorganization and new
combination of academic and vocational curricula. Such an
integrated curriculum would from the first year of high school
begin giving students core knowledge relevant to the human
services. It would in essence make the humanities concretely
pertinent to the needs of modern life and prepare the student
for work in his chosen field immediately upon graduation,
while at the same time enriching him culturally and preparing him to go on to college if he chooses.

With a curriculum that immediately engages the student
in preparing for a realistic future, that develops his self-
knowledge, and that also gives him a broad view of the
cultural continuum of the humanities and its applicability to
his own world and his place in it, it is logical to suppose that
a greater number of students would be motivated to remain
in school until they obtain a diploma.

[5] Arthur Pearl, *op. cit.*

The student would know when he starts his high school program that the courses he takes will lead to jobs for which openings really exist, and that these jobs have built-in opportunities for upward, diagonal, and lateral mobility.

Such a curriculum would extend the meaning of vocational education far beyond the machine-shop and typing classes which now define it. By including all students it would eliminate the elitism of college preparatory programs and the "locking-out" tendency of the vocational courses.

A university education is based on the credo that thorough grounding in the humanities is essential to adequate functioning in a vocation, whether the vocation be business administration, engineering, advertising, or literature. One can predict that in the world of the future the humanities will be increasingly important not only for professionals, but for the paraprofessionals at all levels of human-service work.

According to a study of subprofessionals in a health program at Holyoke Community College in Springfield, Massachusetts, career-oriented systematic education (as opposed to typical vestibule training directed only toward learning a job and performing in it efficiently) *"is not merely preferable but necessary."*

It broadens the trainee's grasp of the significance of his work. An assistant who performs housing or restaurant inspections, or weighs babies, or assists the elderly and infirm, with a knowledge of the socio-political and biological implications of his work, is an assistant immeasurably more valuable to the health service agency than the aide who mechanically follows orders.

The Women's Talent Corps of New York City, which began its operations in 1966 as a trainer of mature undereducated women for work as aides in human-service agencies, discovered that general theoretical knowledge was essential to the training program, and that it was in effect functioning as an academic institution as well as a skill-training center. From this evolved the idea of the Women's Talent Corps Junior College, where the curriculum will combine academic subjects with job practice, making each aspect of the courses more meaningful to the other.

If the value of academic learning at the college and junior

college level of vocational education is beginning to be accepted, would it not be wise to center vocational education in the high school around a strong academic core?

An integrated curriculum oriented toward a multiplicity of career options might include elements of sociology, psychology, group dynamics, economics. It would teach literature, history, and the arts within an explicit social context, reaching the individual directly. Pioneer work in this approach is already being done with effective results:

The Pre-Tech Programs developed by San Francisco State College, which have been in effect for the past six years in 19 Bay Area high schools (in disadvantaged and middle-class communities) feature a core curriculum which relates the traditional academic subjects to the technical vocational goals of the students. For example, Project FEAST prepares students to enter the food and hospitality industries, and meaningfully ties in the study of literature and history to the technological studies.* The mathematical science courses integrate literature with technical writing. The Program aims to give students a salable skill upon graduation, plus the necessary academic background so that he may enter junior college or a university, if he wishes. It is especially geared to under-achievers whose lack of competence in academic subjects results from underdeveloped interest. *It was feared that there would be a watering-down of the classics, but the contrary has been true. As the students' interest has been awakened, they have demanded more and more* knowledge of the humanities.[6]

Those of us accustomed to traditional education and yesterday's vocations must adopt a new point of view. Technical education in the "new" technological society is different. Profound changes have taken place in a relatively few years until, it now seems, the purposes of general education and of technical-vocational education are rapidly converging. They represent two points of view toward accomplishing the same thing. The Pre-Tech English teacher, for example, may use the technical report

* One of the striking facts of Project FEAST is that male students make up more than three-quarters of its enrollment.

[6] Robert S. Craig, Director Pre-Tech Programs (personal communication).

instead of the narrative essay as the most appropriate vehicle to accomplish her purposes. However, this does not mean that she must ignore the cultural aspects of our language. In fact, we would like to think that the inclusion of technology into the cultural portion of any high school English program has validity for all students, traditional or Pre-Tech.[7]

Project ABLE of Quincy, Massachusetts, funded by the U.S. Office of Education, is developing a curriculum to organize vocational training in "families of skills" and to teach academic subjects in relation to those skills. The aim of the new approach is to provide all students (whether they are preparing for college or for a job after high school) with skills immediately salable after graduation. The new vocational-technical high school covers the tenth to the fourteenth year, and plans are to begin vocational training even before the ninth grade. The idea for the project evolved from the discovery that although the overwhelming effort of Massachusetts' public schools is toward college preparation, only 20 percent of high school graduates who enter college have enough commitment to finish.

Mario Fantini and Gerald Weinstein have made cogent suggestions for a "contact curriculum."

Ignore the prescribed units, but not the general subject area and within those subject limits create and develop original units of study. . . :

> History—The Civil Rights Movement
>   The Roots of Conflict
>   The Changing World of Work
> Math—What is "good" money?
> Science—How can we do work easier?
>   What is race?
> Language Arts—How can advertisements fool us?
>   Words and what they do to you.
> Social Studies—What part can we play in politics?
>   Why are rules necessary?

[7] *The Pre-Technology Program, a Descriptive Report,* 1966.

An interdisciplinary problem-solving unit. First isolate the problem, then ask how each subject . . . might contribute toward its solution. Some problems might be:

> Why do people organize?
> What does where I live and who I live with have to do with how I behave?
> Why do people have such trouble in getting along with each other?
> How many ways are there for looking at the same things?
> How are people the same and different from each other?[8]

Fantini and Weinstein suggest a curriculum that is initially experience based, but adds a vertically programmed small-step sequence of skills; it places equal emphasis on cognitive, extrinsic content and on affective, inner content.

Field practice would be an important part of the holistic curriculum, from the beginning. In this Junior Antioch model the students would actually participate in education, recreation, community-development activities with increasing responsibility as they advance in their studies. They would of course receive school credit for their field work. If, as has been proposed by some educators, schools remain in session throughout the year, with no long vacation period, field work would be eminently well suited to such a lengthened term program. But even without the longer terms it may be possible to set up field-work programs during the summer months and after school, with the students being paid for their work. Something along this line is already being done.

> The Homework Helper program of Mobilization for Youth in New York City hires high school youngsters to tutor elementary school youngsters in reading. It has been found that not only did the tutees' reading skills improve, but that the tutors' skills improved even more.

> Chase Manhattan Bank has an after-school training program in banking for potential high school dropouts

[8] *Toward a Contact Curriculum,* Anti-Defamation League of B'nai B'rith, New York City, 1968; Mario Fantini and Gerald Weinstein, *The Disadvantaged: Challenge to Education,* New York, Harper & Row, 1968.

wherein the youths are gaining practical experience in the field, and also earning $1.75 for the work they do as they learn.

A student thinking about education as a career, for example, could gain his field practice and earn an hourly wage by working in after-school child-care projects, or in day camps during the summer. This would help to provide a needed service, and give the student an early and intense first-hand view of the career he contemplates, thus enabling him to make his career choice with valuable foreknowledge.

The human service-oriented curriculum would be integrally connected to the increasing number of New Careers programs developing throughout the nation. Students stepping directly from high school into a New Careers program would thus be assured of continuing education and training on the job, and an institutionalized, visible career-ladder structure for advancement toward professional standing. It is possible that in some of these programs students would start work not at the entry-level position, but at a higher step, since they would already have had some education for the human services and a high school diploma.

In the career program sponsored by the New York City Board of Education, educational auxiliaries with a high school diploma are hired at the assistant level, rather than at the aide entry-level position, and earn correspondingly more.

The integrated curriculum should avoid the locking-in drawbacks of the present curricula. That is, it should not be so exclusively oriented toward the human services that students have no options for entering other fields. With such a course of study it should be possible to become a health worker, or an education worker, or to leave the human-service field entirely and go on to a college program directed toward engineering, if one wishes.

One of the principal objectives of the curriculum should be to contact and hold large numbers of students who see no relevance in present courses by opening to them a wide range of possibilities, more immediate jobs, and course work directly related to these jobs.

One cannot pretend, of course, that there are not many complexities and problems in reorganizing school programs in this way. There is the danger that courses may be watered down so that they become meaningless. It is obvious that the teachers of such curricula would themselves need special orientation and training. There is a danger of distorting traditional subjects or the classics, or of giving them short shrift.

These dangers would have to be carefully guarded against in order to insure that we develop well-educated and motivated recruits for the rapidly growing needy sectors of our service economy.

The importance of building a strong academic backbone into the integrated curriculum proposed here cannot be too much insisted on. The value of a liberal education may be debatable but it is doubtful that the man who functions in the service industries could fulfill his role satisfactorily without some background in the humanities, the sciences, and the social sciences.

VIII

A MENTAL HEALTH STRATEGY: THE NEIGHBORHOOD SERVICE CENTER

PART I

Without arguing the intricacies of the evidence, it seems fairly apparent that low-income populations are not being reached by mental health facilities and that there is considerable need among this population. If we are to come anywhere near filling the gap, it will be necessary to develop and utilize new mental health resources. The traditional clinical psychiatric hospital-based resources are patently inadequate to meet the needs of large segments of the population. What is needed is new manpower, approaches, concepts, as well as more strategic uses of our existing resources. In light of the limitations of present resources, we will have to rethink traditional preventive psychiatry formulations which stress early case finding and rapid referral on the assumption that there is some adequate back-up base that can really assist in reversing crises for large masses of the population. This is simply not true, and before we plan such a program of secondary prevention, we should assess very carefully the available resources and manpower; otherwise, we will quickly substitute evaluation and diagnosis for treatment and develop enormous waiting lists. In a way it is fortunate that mental health facilities have been underutilized by the poor, because if they were adequately used there would not be enough available.

Before turning to see how mental health service can be provided for large segments of the population, it might be useful to say a few words about previous attempts to deal with this problem, particularly efforts at modeling mental health resources for low-income populations. Most of the approaches have been directed toward modifying the form of casework and psychotherapeutic approach so that it will be more consonant with the needs, expectations, and style of low-income populations. Florence Hollis argues that the fundamental casework approach need only be modified slightly in form in order to be congruent with low-income populations.[1] What is being suggested here is that such casework approaches, whatever their modifications, will simply not be sufficient to serve millions of people who need assistance. Casework may not be the intervention of choice even if it could be modified because it would not be able to scratch the surface of the problem and therefore should only be used, like psychotherapy, selectively with certain representatives of low-income populations with particular disturbances.

Here is a brief outline of the potential resources that could be utilized and developed for service to the poor:

(1) Expand the deviance tolerance (acceptability of differences) of low-income populations to include those designated as mentally ill. This tolerance can also be utilized to assist in rehabilitating large numbers of low-income people who are not defined as mentally ill, but in addition it may be possible to transform and extend this deviance tolerance to

[1] "Casework and Social Class," *Social Casework,* October 1965.

include mentally ill people returning from mental institutions. There are any number of ways of achieving this objective—decentralized neighborhood-based centers staffed by nonprofessional personnel who are accepted in the neighborhood, the selected use of formerly ill people who are now recognized as significant leaders in the community. For example, a Father Keogh in Australia's Recovery movement introduces himself to audiences as "I am Father Keogh, formerly deranged." This is very effective for altering the "crazy" stereotype because he makes an excellent appearance and presentation.

(2) Utilize the self-help agencies such as AA, Recovery, Inc., Synanon, Schizophrenics Anonymous, Gamblers Anonymous, and so on. Bring these agencies into low-income communities where they typically do not exist, and, probably more important, tie them in with professional resources in the community.

(3) Utilize and strengthen the informal leaders who have some feeling for people in trouble.

(4) Use and expand the new nonprofessional manpower. Nonprofessionals seem excellent at peer intervention and there is increasing evidence that this type of intervention, while different from professional intervention, has a significant effectiveness in all social classes. This is illustrated in group therapy and in the self-help groups. Nonprofessionals can more effectively and appropriately use subjectivity and can be judgmental within limits. They are also very helpful in providing support, reducing isolation, assisting catharsis and objectification, and they are very able at persuasion and community organization.

(5) Utilize large numbers of noncredentialed personnel—graduate students, housewives, Peace Corps returnees. These groups, like the nonprofessionals, can be trained to utilize their particular potentialities (their nonprofessional selves) and can increase their skills through training.

(6) Reconceptualize, so that treatment can be envisioned at a distance. Improvement in disorders can occur through social involvement, through changing the cohesion of the neighborhood and reducing the isolation of people. Alexander Leighton's findings in rural communities provide powerful support for the possibility that pathology can be reduced through social measures aimed at utilizing the strengths of

the community, increasing its cohesion and integration. These sociotherapeutic approaches should not simply be described as nonspecific primary prevention; they also function as treatment, as Leighton's evidence indicates.

(7) Develop helpers in the community from those who were formerly in need.[2] People get better through helping others.

(8) Use professional resources more strategically for training, consulting, and supervisory purposes, as well as for specialized evaluation and treatment.

(9) Professional technology must be expanded to include new group approaches to low-income populations, such as greater utilization of role-playing, etc.

(10) Mental health approaches can be provided under many auspices; trade unions, churches, settlement houses, and so on. The exclusive direction of these programs by medical leadership, utilizing the medical model, is constraining. Many of the concepts discussed above have not arisen from traditional psychiatric and medical theory and their application should not be exclusively in the hands of this leadership.

The need for the expansion of services in relation to everyday living problems is extremely important in reducing crises, stress, emergencies, and providing the necessary support that will reduce isolation and anxiety. Similarly, the importance of parties, socials—the mobilization of joy in the community— is extremely important in reducing isolation and as an added therapeutic arm.

The development of positive mental health should not be seen as isolated from the reduction and control of pathology or negative mental health. Approaches directed toward controlling contagion of disturbance should be carefully considered, particularly in light of the usual emphasis on returning ill people to the community as quickly as possible for rehabilitation.

[2] See F. Riessman, "The Helper Therapy Principle," *Social Work*, April 1965.

PART II

with Emanuel Hallowitz

One of the most effective strategies for dealing with the problems of mental health is the Neighborhood Service Center. It is an innovative structure directed toward providing a more effective approach to low-income people in a highly disadvantaged area in the South Bronx, New York City. The present program is a product of the cross-fertilization of two distinct orientations: preventive psychiatry (1) and community action. Its unique features include staffing by indigenous nonprofessionals (supervised by professionals), a mental health orientation, and the uniting of service and community action in a carefully phased sequence.

Three neighborhood service centers were developed under the auspices of Lincoln Hospital Mental Health Services in 1965.[1] The development of these centers was based upon the view that an effective community mental health program must not only provide direct assistance to those whose pathology has reached critical proportions, but it must also identify and support those forces in the community that are conducive to development of mental health and combat those community forces that are destructive to the mental well-being of the community's inhabitants.

The neighborhood service center program arises from combining this orientation with knowledge about low-income communities; e.g., voluntary family and children's services are meager and scattered in disadvantaged areas; fragmented public services often present a frustrating network of barriers; traditional ways of operating (waiting lists, weekly appointments, long-term service, and emphasis on "talking through") are not consonant with the needs, experience, or life style of

[1] For a description of the Lincoln Hospital Mental Health Services see (7).

low-income people.

Each of the three neighborhood service centers that were established in 1965 is located in an area characterized by a high density of pathology—psychiatric, social, and economic. They are called neighborhood service centers, not mental health centers, by design. These centers provide an opportunity for anyone in the neighborhood with whatever kind of problem or trouble to walk in and talk immediately to someone about his concerns and to get some degree of help. No appointments are required and there are no waiting lists. The first contact is not with the receptionist but directly with the indigenous nonprofessional, who is the main service agent.

This allows residents the possibility of receiving immediate aid and comfort without having to define their problems in a way appropriate to the help-saving system. Immediate assistance is thus furnished before the problem worsens and develops into less reversible pathology. Moreover, the fact that the center is located in the midst of the neighborhood it is to serve provides a visibility and relatedness to the community. In addition, the employment of neighborhood residents (indigenous nonprofessionals), their naturalness, and the informal atmosphere of the setting confirm the "open door" policy and enable freer contact and communication on the part of "clients" from the area.

The problems that are brought to the neighborhood service center run the gamut of human misery, from helping a resident make application to a housing project to requests for assistance in more complex and stressful situations such as aiding a parent accept the need for service to a retarded child, helping a family threatened with eviction, assisting a pregnant unmarried girl and her family to secure appropriate services, and helping a resident to accept and obtain needed psychiatric services.

In some cases on-the-spot advice and guidance are sufficient. In others, giving information as to where needed services can be obtained is all that is required; but more usually, the seeker of service must be helped to know how to deal with bottlenecks or red tape and may need the encouragement and support of the nonprofessional worker in order to maintain motivation, dignity, and self-esteem. In some cases the services required are not readily available (waiting lists) and the neighborhood service center worker is called upon to engage in a "holding action"—to use his knowledge and skill to keep a crisis situation from deteriorating further.

The major goals of the neighborhood service center program are: 1) to provide psychosocial first aid for large numbers of people experiencing stress from both external and internal causes; 2) to transform clients into helpers[2] and active citizens; 3) to develop independence, autonomy, and better functioning on the part of the people in the community; 4) to demonstrate that indigenous nonprofessionals under professional supervision can be trained to provide meaningful service for a disadvantaged population;[3] 5) to initiate changes in relation to the service-giving practices of the agencies in the community; the neighborhood service center is seen as a significant unit that can serve as a hub around which various existing services can be coordinated to facilitate continuity of care; 6) to affect the community life of the area by developing greater social integration and cohesion.

PSYCHOSOCIAL FIRST AID

The central role of the neighborhood service center is that of a "psychosocial first aid station." The psychosocial first aid includes giving information, providing simple advice and counseling, expediting services from other agencies, and environmental manipulation. Through assisting in reducing the number of life stresses encountered in everyday living and by aiding individuals to cope with their overwhelming problems, the center provides an essential mental health service.

Langner and associates (4) document the view that psychiatric disturbance is related to the number of stresses operative upon the individual. Thus a program designed to reduce stresses should have important implications for mental health, both in the reduction of pathology and in the increase of positive mental health (3).

---

[2] The use of the helper principle may be of special importance. Here people are consciously placed in a helper role not only to help other people, but for the development of the helper himself by increasing his coping ability, self-image, etc. See (8).

[3] For a discussion of nonprofessionals in community mental health programs, see (6).

In this connection Fried notes that the effects of deprivation on psychopathology may be modified if there is

1) the sense of security in the availability of resources during crises of transition; 2) actual assistance (economic aid, advice, homemaker service) of various types to compensate for deficits in temporary crises of deprivation or disruption; 3) implicit and explicit encouragement to reorganize psychological resources either through group denial of hopelessness or through ego support by clarifying alternatives (2).

The fact that the resident can enter the mental health service system through the neighborhood service center without having to define his concerns in psychiatric language may enable the problems to be dealt with before they become symptoms; the client need not develop symptomatology in order to receive aid nor does he have to label his difficulties as sickness or mental problems. Low-income clients, in particular, have not been responsive to such labeling. Being defined as sick has regressive consequences for all classes, and to the extent that the client can be assisted in his problem without having it defined as sickness, to that extent are the ego-weakening properties reduced.[4] The very nature of the neighborhood service center may enable the individual to define his problem in a more everyday fashion (as problems of living) and to be less apt to conceive of himself as ill.

The neighborhood service center program aims to provide psychosocial first aid and counseling of a simple type. This "counseling" consists largely of providing a listening ear and some emotional support. The skills involved are based on enlarging the friendliness and warmth believed to be characteristic of the neighborhood worker's style. The nonprofessional's basic pattern of relationship is not "trained out." The

[4] Caplan states: "In many cases, a quicker and better result might be obtained if this ego weakening could be avoided by defining the role of the deviant in such a way that his self-respect, mature status, and responsibility were not reduced; for instance, if he were categorized as a person grappling with material hazards and challenges; one engaged in social readjustment; one dealing with parental, educational, or religious tasks. Each of these roles involves the expectation of strain, frustration, of occasional perplexity and conflict; but in each of them, although the person may solicit the assistance and support of others, he is expected to act his age and to behave in conformity with normal social standards" (1).

mental health aide is made aware of the fact that in providing all types of concrete service, it is important for him to enable the client to talk fully and freely about his problems and to furnish him the personal emotional support that is so valuable. Hence, a psychological service is built in as a concomitant of most other services.

An important dimension in furnishing service at the neighborhood service center is to have the nonprofessional mental health aide provide an appropriate model to the client or "customer." It would be very easy for the aide to encourage the client to become dependent upon service. On the contrary, the program encourages the client to become involved in a mutual and reciprocal relationship with other people who are also in need of help. People are encouraged to help each other and not simply to receive help.

The aide has to be trained to present this model and to encourage this form of interaction and development. He has to be constantly on the alert to transform "helpees" into helpers, and basic community norms that emphasize commonality, mutuality, and reciprocity must be built. In a sense, an effort is made to develop a "therapeutic community."

It should be borne in mind that as significant and meaningful as it may be, the provision of psychosocial first aid through the neighborhood service centers is not seen as the sole aim, but also as a vehicle for intervention in community mental health issues. In facilitating services for residents from a variety of social agencies and institutions, the aides come in intimate contact with deliverers of service and particularly lower-echelon management. They have a twofold focus in working with these personnel: 1) to insure that the resident receives adequate service and, 2) to enlarge the perspective of the agents of the traditional institution to increase their understanding of the unique needs, attitudes, and values of the resident population.

In this manner, although the policies of the institutions may not be directly or immediately changed, it is hoped that the manner in which the policies are implemented and the quality of the services rendered will be affected. While the aides are functioning in this direction, the professionals of the neighborhood service center and the professionals of the Lincoln Hospital Mental Health Services are working with higher-echelon staff of these agencies and institutions, attempting to affect policies and practices at this level.

Because the neighborhood service center has become the place in the community to which residents turn in time of crisis, the center is able to keep abreast of the kinds of psycho-social problems with which the residents have to cope, the services needed and their availability. Likewise, the gaps, limitations, and deficiencies in the formal service structure and in the informal alternative arrangements currently employed by the community are detected more readily. Thus the center is an important source of information on the nature of social changes needed, as well as a possible focus from which action to implement the needed changes can arise. The center also plays an important role in finding and developing indigenous leadership and involving those residents in the community who are usually not reached by other social action groups. The neighborhood service center organizes and conducts campaigns, voter registration drives, and health campaigns and disseminates information on job opportunities, planned parenthood, and use of surplus foods.

Users of service and their neighbors are invited to community meetings in which an attempt is made to identify some of the major community problems and to organize action committees. For example, there is a hospital committee, welfare committee, tenants' association, block association, etc.

The aim in organizing such groups and programs is to develop a more competent and cohesive community. Leighton notes that more integrated communities appear to be less subject to mental stress and mental illness.

> . . . it is significant that the prevalence of (psychiatric) disorders on the Road was far lower in 1962 than it had been in 1952. . . . Improvement in mental health closely paralleled the growing integration of the community. Conversely, other communities that were disintegrated in 1962 have shown no comparable decline in the prevalence of psychiatric disorder (5) .

The neighborhood service center program endeavors to produce a cohesive community by utilizing the inherent strengths of the neighborhood and building upon them, rather than assuming that the neighborhood consists simply of pathology and isolation. It is hypothesized that if people can be involved in taking action in their own behalf, this will counteract feelings of despair and apathy and support feelings of autonomy and power. For some it may even provide healthy sublimation and thus contribute further to positive mental health.

While the major emphasis of the neighborhood service center program is directed toward primary prevention, the program is also concerned with secondary and tertiary prevention. One center is planning for the utilization of a room as a meeting place for "keep-in-touch" clubs for patients who return to the area. Some of the aides will be trained specifically to work with these people and to assist in their rehabilitation, helping them to return to their families in the community. In their in-service training the aides receive assistance in detecting disturbances in clients, referring them to the Lincoln Hospital Mental Health Clinic when necessary and assisting with holding measures.

PRELIMINARY RESULTS

From February 22, 1965, when the first center opened, to December 31 of that year, 7,119 different people were served by two of the centers. (Statistics for the third center have been excluded since the center did not begin operations until the last week of December.) During the six-month period (July-December) when both centers were in full operation, 6,620 new cases came for service—an average of 1,037 cases per month.

Projecting these figures for a full year's operation gives a total of 6,220 individuals per year per center. The size of the average family coming to the center is 3.9. Thus, it is not unreasonable to state that indirectly, each center touches the lives of some 25,000 people, and this does not include the many hundreds more who have become involved with the center through the various community education and action campaigns.

Based on these statistics, it appears that the neighborhood service center unit is an excellent device for reaching a large proportion of the residents in the area it is designated to serve. Although experience with the centers is limited, findings to date are most encouraging. It seems fairly clear that nonprofessionals can provide and expedite service for large numbers of disadvantaged families. Moreover, it is evident that nonprofessionals can intervene in critical situations, engage comparatively pathological people in meaningful relationships, stimulate them to take action in their own behalf, mobilize community resources, and serve as a bridge between the client in need and the professional service. The nonprofessional is able to perform some tasks that are usually carried out by professionals but really do not require professional training and experience. In this manner the outreach of the professional service is expanded and considerably more people can be affected than would be possible by using professional personnel alone.

The aides and the professional staff have established good relations with the various agencies in the community and have obtained considerable cooperation from them in relation to service delivery. While the neighborhood service center program has been able to influence the practice of some agency workers, it has not had any impact as yet on overall agency practices and policies. However, some of the group-serving agencies—the settlement houses and the churches—and the health agencies have evinced some interest in utilizing nonprofessionals and establishing small neighborhood service center units. They have apparently been influenced by the neighborhood service center model and have requested assistance from the program in expanding in these new directions.

The aides also serve as effective role models for people in the community. Many of them have become active in their own buildings and neighborhoods, assisting neighbors and friends with personal problems and participating in organizations devoted to improving neighborhood conditions. Both in their private life and in their job life, they have been able to provide some degree of community leadership. They have organized delegations to appear at public hearings, at times have been spokesmen for these groups, and at other times have helped others to take leadership.

It would be difficult to enumerate all the problems that have been encountered: for example, selecting personnel, both nonprofessional and professional; developing appropriate training programs for nonprofessionals and professionals (content, timing, dosage) ; redefining roles of the nonprofessional and the professional; assisting in the emotional readjustment required of each group (professional and nonprofessional) to fully assume a new role; developing guidelines for determining priorities or program choices that will take into account intensity of needs, skills of worker, pacing, timing, conflicting demands, etc.; and above all, articulating this program of neighborhood service centers with the other programs of Lincoln Hospital Mental Health Services so that there is truly a comprehensive network of community mental health service rather than disparate, fragmented units of service.

CONCLUSION

The neighborhood service center may be a central feature in the community mental health centers which will be proliferating throughout the country. Not only can it reach neighborhood populations, but it can serve to bring together hospital-based clinical services, agency-based social services, and informally organized community help.

The project appears to be demonstrating that nonprofessionals under professional supervision can assist clients by providing direct service and psychological support. It also seems to indicate that a neighborhood service center unit can furnish a remarkable amount of service coverage for the 50,000 people in its designated area of service. The possibility of the neighborhood service center as a basic unit from which many different types of program can be launched merits investigation. The center appears to be a potential base for involving the community, for holding block ("town") meetings, and for transforming clients into neighborhood service center members, but these remain largely possibilities at this point, awaiting exploration.

REFERENCES

1. G. Caplan, *Principles of Preventive Psychiatry*, New York, Basic Books, 1964.
2. M. Fried, "Social Problems and Psychopathology," in Group for the Advancement of Psychiatry: Urban America and the Planning of Mental Health Services, Symposium No. 10. New York, Group for the Advancement of Psychiatry, 1964, pp. 430-431.

3. M. Jahoda, *Current Concepts of Positive Mental Health,* New York, Basic Books, 1958.

4. T. Langner, *Life Stress and Mental Health,* New York, The Free Press (Macmillan), 1963, pp. 466-467.

5. A. Leighton, "Poverty and Social Change," *Scientific American,* 212:21-27, 1965.

6. A. Pearl and F. Riessman, *New Careers for the Poor,* New York, The Free Press (Macmillan), 1965, ch. 5.

7. H. Peck, S. Kaplan, and M. Rowan, "Prevention, Treatment and Social Action: A Strategy of Intervention in a Disadvantaged Urban Area," *Amer. J. Orthopsychiat.,* 36:57-69, 1966.

8. F. Riessman, "The 'Helper' Therapy Principle," *Social Work,* 10:27-32, 1965.

CHAPTER

TRAINING THE
NONPROFESSIONAL

N onprofessionals are being utilized in a number of different structures. One major model is the neighborhood service center. This may be a storefront, employing five to ten nonprofessionals with one or two supervisors, which was the pattern at the Lincoln Project described in Chapter VIII (Hallowitz & Riessman, 1966), or the larger multiservice neighborhood centers, which may include anywhere from thirty to two hundred nonprofessionals with a professional staff of five to thirty supervisors.

This model is characterized by a high ratio of nonprofessionals to professionals and a base of operation in the community, on the "home turf," so to speak, of the nonprofessional. The character of the involvement of the NP is likely to be quite different from the second model. Here the NP is attached to a service agency, such as the Welfare Department or the Health Department. He is not in the majority and his base of operations is not in the community but rather in the agency itself. Some of these agencies may be committed to an ideology emphasizing the value and significant new role of the nonprofessional, but in other cases they may simply be utilizing the new manpower because of the assistance it provides to professionals or because funding was available for NP positions.

Thus the variables to be considered are: the ratio of professionals to nonprofessionals; the base of operation, whether it be in the community or in the traditional agency; and the ideology or lack of it connected to the utilization of this new type of personnel. Training and supervisory staff should consider these three dimensions as they have implications for training methodology and supervision and for the development of the nonprofessional, the role he can play, his participation, and his power.

PHASED TRAINING

The relationship of training to job performance for the nonprofessional is different than it is for other types of employees. Perhaps the main reason for this is the general lack of skill the nonprofessional possesses and, more particularly, the lack of certain requisite skills for the new jobs (*e.g.,* recordkeeping).

The traditional principle that long periods of training are necessary before an individual can be employed must be reversed; the motto should be "Jobs First—Training Built In."

It has become axiomatic that most of the training of the nonprofessional will take place on the job itself. This requires that job functions be phased in slowly and that the NP's receive ample time to master the required tasks at each stage before going on to more advanced tasks.

Prejob training (to be distinguished from core training or the training in basic knowledge which can take place throughout the program) should be oriented primarily to enabling the NP to perform the simplest entry features of the job in a fairly adequate fashion. Moreover, the job itself must be broken down and phased in, so that in the initial stage the nonprofessional will be required to perform only limited aspects of the job itself. Further skills will be learned on the job itself, through on-the-job training and systematic in-service training.

The preservice period should be short, lest anxiety be built up and the aide feel threatened by the anticipated job. The learning should be active, the aide should be doing things; and knowledge and concepts should be brought in around the discussion of his activities.

As quickly as possible the aide should be placed on the job itself for a part of the day under close professional supervision. The sooner the aides can get their feet wet, the better they will feel. Thus, in the Lincoln Project, the aides were placed on the job in the Neighborhood Service Center for half a day in this prejob period (after a three-week period spent in job simulation, practice, etc.). The half-day in which they were not working was utilized to discuss the specific experiences they were having.

Beyond this point, the really significant training and learning will occur on the job itself and in carefully planned discussion about the work they are doing. It is not to be assumed, unlike many other positions, that the NP knows his job when he begins it. Rather, in the early stages of this on-the-job experience, he is actually involved in continuous training, and the first job operations are to be considered preliminary aspects of the position that he will ultimately fulfill. He is really still in training on the job itself.

ON-THE-JOB TRAINING

On-the-job training, then, becomes decisive, and different types of on-the-job training should be considered. The aides will learn from simply performing some of the tasks—that is, they will learn from each other (utilizing peer learning and the helper principle); the aides will learn from their supervisor, who will support them and correct their mistakes and provide assistance at any time on request. The aides will also learn from a special series of group meetings that can be held. One such group can be concerned with systematic training introducing, for example, further skills in interviewing. There can also be group discussions about general problems being experienced: on-the-job problems with professionals, problems with other agencies, problems about their own marginality, problems stemming from competition with each other or annoyance with the type of supervision they are receiving. These discussions should be task centered, with personality and individual components coming in as relevant (the traditional sensitivity training—T group—experience seems to require considerable modification if it is to be used with the nonprofessional population).

Another very significant type of informal training can be developed as the program of the agency moves forward. In the Lincoln NSC program the initial phase was concerned with providing and expediting service. After a number of months the program moved toward the development of groups, committees, community action, campaigns (voter registration, etc.). At this point the program had to be discussed with the aides, and this provided an excellent opportunity for the introduction of new training with regard to concepts and skills. Thus, in order to involve clients in a community meeting, it was necessary to discuss with the aides plans for calling such a meeting, how to conduct the meeting, how to bring the client population to the meeting, how to develop committees, and so on.

The discussion, which was program centered for the most part, brought in training in what might be described as an informal but highly functional fashion. But it is exactly in this fashion that the aides seemed to learn best. They needed to know how to conduct a meeting, develop participation in committees, and the like, and consequently their motivation was high and the learning was sensitive and highly directed. Moreover, such issues as how fast can we move? what kinds of action can we take? what is our relationship to the community? became commonplace discussion, and the concepts and goals of the program were easily introduced in this context. For example, one of the aides asked why we couldn't use an Alinsky-type TWO program approach. Other aides suggested that if we did, we wouldn't have our jobs long. The leader indicated that there were target populations among the poor whom the Alinsky groups did not influence easily but that our agency, because of its legitimacy, might be able to work with and involve in various types of nonmilitant activity. A great deal of excited discussion took place and apparently much concrete understanding regarding the agency's viewpoint emerged.

To take another example: at one of the community meetings that was called, where over a hundred people from the neighborhood attended, the combined enthusiasm of the aides who led the meeting and the client-citizens who attended it went into the formation of eight different committees. In a discussion after the meeting the aides were able to understand fairly easily that they had really run ahead of themselves; that they had taken on more work than the agency could handle. Various methods for consolidating the committees and developing volunteers were then discussed in a highly meaningful fashion. Thus the fact that the programs of the new neighborhood service centers are not fully developed can be used to good advantage in the phasing of the training of the nonprofessionals. As these programs develop, new training appropriate to the program phase can be introduced, and this is a most meaningful way for the aides to learn.

The Howard Community Apprentice Program provides another illustration of functional learning. Initially the functionally illiterate research aides in the Howard Program interviewed each other with a tape recorder and learned only the simplest principles of interviewing in order to perform this task. Before long, they recognized that they needed to know something about how to record this information and categorize it, and later they needed some statistics in order to analyze it appropriately. As each of these needs became apparent, the appropriate training was introduced to develop the requisite skills. This can be done either formally or informally, through systematic in-service training and/or through informal discussions related to the problem.

HOW TO UNIFY TRAINING AND SUPERVISION

When possible, it seems useful to have one person responsible for selecting the aide (interviewing him either individually or in a group), training him, and supervising him in the actual program. This was the model developed by Mary Dowery at the Mobilization for Youth Parent Education Program. It allowed for identification by the aides with one person and prevented the confusion that develops when there are multiple leaders. The limitations in this type of model relate to the fact that one person cannot encompass all the required skills that are to be imparted to the NP's. This difficulty can be minimized to some degree by introducing a number of different consultants as assistants to the trainer at various points. However, the trainer has to utilize this information selectively and interpret to the aides what the consultant is offering. The consultant does not become the leader.

However, in the larger agency model, it will not be as easy for one person to play the multiple roles of selector, trainer, and supervisor. For this model a number of adaptations are recommended.

NP's can be introduced in a circumscribed sphere of the agency—in one department, for example, where the selection, training, and supervisory responsibilities are delegated to one person or to a team of two or three individuals working closely together.

Another possibility is to permit professionals in the larger agency to volunteer to select and work with a nonprofessional assistant, in a sense, functioning as selector, trainer, and supervisor. While some general suggestions can be offered as to how the professionals might use the nonprofessionals, in general it would seem best at this stage to permit the professionals to define the assignments and working relationships. Some professionals will want the NP's, at least at first, to do fairly menial tasks, simply serving as assistants. Others may suggest fairly early that nonprofessionals perform new and meaningful assignments, really discussing things with clients, for example, rather than merely serving as translators. It should be especially valuable for the nonprofessional to work with the professional on a one-to-one basis initially, rather than being involved in a team in which the professionals are the majority.

The professionals who self-select themselves might meet together from time to time with an individual in the organization or a consultant who has responsibility for the development of the use of nonprofessionals—this could be a trainer or other program developer. In these discussions some of the experiences of the professionals would be exchanged and discussed, problems would be raised, and the specialist or consultant would offer advice, bring in experience from other settings, suggest problems that might arise, indicate different roles that nonprofessionals could play.

This way of involving professionals might be an excellent way in which to introduce the nonprofessionals into a particular institution and establish the tradition of using NP's. The resistance on the part of the professionals who did not self-select themselves for working with nonprofessionals might be dissipated after they observed some of the initial (hopefully) positive experiences of the professionals who volunteered.

In the multiservice centers where large numbers of NP's· are to be employed, it will not be possible to integrate the selection, training, and supervisory functions in one individual or small team. To obtain a more full and systematic training product it is probably best to have the training done by a special training agency. Even though a large part of the training will have to be on the job itself, the training organization can dispatch its senior trainers to the service agency in order to provide the initial on-the-job training. (The training institution can provide prejob training at its own base.) The training agency will, of course, have to work very closely with the service organization and plan to phase out its own role, leaving in its place a training and supervisory capability.

RECOMMENDATIONS

(1) Trainers should not expect or demand deep identification with the poor on the part of nonprofessionals, and they should anticipate competitive feelings toward professionals (often professionals other than themselves, but not always).

(2) Constant support and assistance must be provided; supervisors should be available for assistance at all times, and it should be clear to the NP that he can request help without any negative implications regarding his evaluation. (Frequently NP's confuse supervisors with factory foremen.) On the other hand, opportunity for considerable initiative and flexibility on the part of the NP must be established. He wants both the flexibility and the support. He is a new kind of employee, and reflecting the developing antipoverty ideology, he wants more of a say, or at least wants to be consulted, regarding the operation of various programs and rules.

(3) The process of obtaining the job must be made as simple and short as possible. Every effort should be made to reduce the competitive feelings that the recruits may develop in relation to other candidates for the position. Long delays between the original time of the job application and later

interviews are likely to produce considerable anxiety for the candidate. This attitude may be carried over in the training and on the job itself, thus producing competitive difficulties with other aides and anger toward the program and the staff.

(4) The group interview can be used very successfully in selecting applicants. Aside from the fact that it is economical in time, the group process permits the selector to observe how the candidates relate to other people in a group; who influences whom; who listens; who is sensitive; who is overwhelmed by group pressure; who has leadership potential, etc. It is also possible to produce an excellent group atmosphere and develop the beginnings of later camaraderie, *esprit de corps,* group feeling, teamwork, etc. The danger, however, lies in the competitive setting in which the applicants observe that they have to compete against others for a limited number of jobs.

The competitive troubles can be reduced by establishing an informal, friendly setting; coffee and cake should be supplied from the beginning, even before the group forms and starts to talk. A leisurely pace of discussion can be established by the leader or the co-leader. Everybody should be introduced. Plenty of time for warming up should be available. The group should be no larger than ten people and should be sitting fairly close together in a circle or around a table. But the selectors must make perfectly clear that evaluation is taking place and that it will be difficult to assess people unless they participate and have something to say. Otherwise "quiet ones" will be penalized by this group selection process. The group session itself should stress interaction and not go around the circle having each person announce his interests or goals.

(5) Nonprofessionals frequently expect magic from the training process; that is, they expect to learn how to do everything they are supposed to do quite perfectly. To the degree that this is not achieved, they blame the training process. To some extent this reflects a naïve view about training, education, and learning. The training staff should be aware that it probably will receive this reaction and insofar as possible should try to explain to the trainees that many dimensions of the job will take some time to learn fully in practice. Fundamentally, of course, the trainees' reaction reflects their anxiety about the new job and role and this has to be dealt with in

other ways as indicated below. Trainers also sometimes expect too much from the training; sometimes their expectations of nonprofessionals are initially too high and their appraisal of adequate progress is based on experience with more experienced professional learners. While NP's have some surprising knowledge and understanding of a variety of issues, there are areas of their knowledge that are unbelievably remiss. They often have great gaps in their knowledge or know-how about the system—how to fill out forms, how to make outlines, how to take tests, how to read effectively. Because they are frequently very sensitive and bright in their understanding of people and the neighborhood, the tendency (in halo fashion) is to assume that their understanding is equally good in areas removed from their previous experience. Thus, it is a shock to discover that a nonprofessional who has conducted an excellent interview with a client records the interview inadequately. Constant training and emphasis must be built in to improve report-writing skills, etc.

(6) Nonprofessionals have quickly learned that part of the ideology of the antipoverty movement is directed toward developing, not merely jobs for nonprofessionals, but career lines as well. It is therefore extremely important that the agency establish these lines so that there can be aides, assistants, associates, supervisory positions, and possibly assistant neighborhood service center director positions available to the nonprofessional through career development and education. The training staff must clarify these career lines, indicating the relationship of education to them and further indicating the time involved before individuals can expect to "move up." If this is not done appropriately, aspirations may develop very rapidly and may outstrip possibilities.

(7) Nonprofessionals should be encouraged as soon as possible to form their own groups or unions. (We would predict that organization and unionization of the aides will progress fairly rapidly in the coming period.) Aides at Harlem Hospital have been encouraged to meet by themselves, but these meetings have been recorded and utilized by the research staff there. The Lincoln aides meet independently at an "aides-only" meeting, not under the surveillance of their professional supervisors. These groups are very important in developing the power of the aides and a feeling of identification as a

group and should contribute greatly to the formation of role identity and job identity. In the Lincoln Project aides also met off the job on their own time. These meetings led to the development of leadership among the aides, to powerful group identity vis-à-vis the professionals on the staff, and to the raising of a number of highly significant demands: the demand for greater participation in certain aspects of decision making of the organization (this was not an unlimited demand for participation on all decisions) ; the demand for closer supervision and periodic discussions with the leaders of the program; the curtailment of T groups (sensitivity training groups, which were highly unpopular among the aides) ; the demand for career lines to be developed so that nonprofessionals could move up the ladder—the associated demand for education to be provided by the Yeshiva University, of which the Lincoln Project is a part; the demand that if volunteers were to be used, they should be carefully trained; the demand for a greater voice in the selection of delegates to the local Anti-Poverty Community Convention, the request for the aides-only meeting.

(8) While much emphasis has been placed on the use of group procedures in training, it should be noted that a great deal of deep learning develops on a one-to-one identification basis. Bank Street College's summer experiment, in which each teacher worked one hour per day with one student, found this one of the most effective learning devices. And Mobilization for Youth's homework-helper program, in which one high school youngster worked individually with one elementary school youngster, also supports the value of the one-to-one relationship. This principle can be utilized at a number of points in the training design. As noted above, individual aides can be assigned to professionals in the agency who select themselves for this purpose and volunteer to develop a nonprofessional assistant. We have also found that it is possible to use experienced, trained nonprofessionals to assist in one-to-one work with new trainees; that is, for a period during the day a new trainee can be assigned to work alongside an experienced nonprofessional. This has to be done selectively or else we will have the blind leading the blind. But when it is supervised thoroughly, the possibility of utilizing the full advantages of peer learning exists. Peers learn from each

other in very different ways and sometimes more fully than they learn from "superior" teachers. The helper principle notes that the peer teacher (that is, the more advanced aide) learns enormously from imparting information to the trainee; he learns from teaching (Riessman, 1965).

(9) While a certain degree of anxiety is useful in stimulating learning, the NP is probably faced by far too much anxiety due to his ambiguous role. Hence, every effort should be made to reduce the anxiety level. This can be achieved by phasing of tasks (not demanding too much too fast), defining the job as carefully as possible, developing group support, providing specific training and evaluation (positive performance should be commended in as detailed a fashion as are weaknesses), providing constant supervisory support and assistance, and holding frank discussions of program and role difficulties. We suspect that the NP's anxiety tolerance is not high and that a learning style that utilizes anxiety stimulation is not characteristic of this population.

(10) Many professionals express great concern about nonprofessionals losing their community ties, their feeling for the neighborhood, and their identification with "the people." This is based on the obvious fact that nonprofessionals are no longer simply members of the community but are now employed by an agency. Moreover, since career lines may develop, the NP's can anticipate moving up the ladder, and, in some cases, becoming professionals.

The issue is not whether the NP identifies with the poor or not, but rather whether he remains committed to them. (Many professionals are committed to the poor without in any way identifying with this population.) What the antipoverty program needs from the indigenous nonprofessional is his knowledge, his ability to communicate with the poor, and his commitment. It does not need his identification with the poor.

Actually, it generally takes people a long time to lose their knowledge and understanding of the ways, traditions, style, and language of their origin. And if they initially have some commitment, this concern will not fall away overnight. Thus, the commitment and knowledge can remain even if immediate identification diminishes. Moreover, commitment can be maintained by the reinforcement of it by the agency and the training staff. In other words, to the extent that the agency reflects the developing antipoverty ideology, it can reinforce and reward at every turn the nonprofessional's concern for his neighborhood and the poor. The training staff can be critical of any tendency on the part of the nonprofessionals to lose this commitment as they come to identify with the agency or with professionals. In other words, it is possible for nonprofessionals to develop new identifications, at the same time maintaining traditional commitments. In fact these commitments can be deepened by new systematic understanding regarding the nature of poverty. It is in this context that continuous training can perhaps provide its greatest contribution to the nonprofessional and the antipoverty program.

REFERENCES

E. Hallowitz and F. Riessman, "The Role of the Indigenous Nonprofessional in a Community Mental Health Neighborhood Service Center Program." Paper presented at the American Orthopsychiatric Association, San Francisco, April 15, 1966.

A. Pearl and F. Riessman, *New Careers for the Poor*, New York, Free Press, 1965.

F. Riessman, "The Helper Therapy Principle," *Social Work*, Vol. 10, No. 2, April 1965, pp. 27-31.

X

BIRTH CONTROL, CULTURE, AND THE POOR

Catherine Kohler Riessman

For the first time in the United States, religious and related political pressures are relaxing in the area of birth control and it is now being explored as a matter of public policy.

In terms of the sociology of knowledge it is interesting to note that the current trend is toward increasing birth control services for every branch of the society, not only the middle class. The extension of this health service to the poor on a massive scale is being seriously pondered on a national level. Economically, large families are no longer beneficial to the country or the family. Child labor laws and the industrial age have made obsolete the usefulness of offspring as members of the labor force. The industrialization of agriculture similarly removes the need of child labor, historically used on the small family farm. Unemployment among youth is at an all-time high, many times greater than the proportional rate among the adult categories.

Thus it might be hypothesized that the new economic conditions, making it no longer functional to have large families, have given rise to increased research into and concrete plans for implementation of birth control services, particularly in the population group most burdened by many children—the poor. In addition to the economic factors reinforcing this change in emphasis, we now have the physical technologies to do the job effectively. The oral contraceptives and the intrauterine devices (IUD) have made the question of birth control largely a social one. Medically, the techniques are highly developed and nearly 100 percent effective. Perhaps the rapid development of these techniques is not unrelated to the changing economic conditions. Moreover, the antipoverty program, although hesitantly, is venturing into this area, and has funded a number of programs. With the addition of Medicare, the opportunity for delivering the necessary services to the poor on a massive scale is within our grasp for the first time.[1] Can we simply make the techniques of contraception available to this group as they have been to the middle class? Is it enough to provide the service or must we plan a program specifically tailored to this population, taking into consideration the attitudes and cultural patterns likely to be encountered?

First and foremost, what is the attitude of the low-income family toward birth control? Are we likely to encounter deep "cultural" resistance to the idea of limiting family size on religious or value grounds? A study conducted in 1955, using a national sample of 2,713 white married women in childbearing years, shows that women of all classes want to limit their families.[2] Employing the same data, Lee Rainwater showed that young women of all classes appear to *want* the

[1] Howard A. Rusk, M.D., "Birth Control as Policy," *New York Times,* May 15, 1966, p. 74.

[2] R. Freedman, P. K. Whelpton, A. Campbell, *Family Planning, Sterility and Population Growth,* New York, McGraw-Hill, Inc., 1959, p. 40.

same number of children (2 to 4) .[3] The goal, then, appears to remain constant regardless of class. The actual births and the expectation, however, vary with class. "The lower the status (as measured most effectively in this study by the wife's education) , the more children the respondents have, and the more they expect."[4] Predictably, the lower the status of the woman, the more children expected; the women with only a grammar school education showed the higher fertility pattern.[5]

COITUS-CONNECTED
METHODS OF BIRTH CONTROL

Perhaps the significance of cultural factors can best be understood in relation to low-income attitudes toward the traditional *coitus-connected* (*e.g.,* condom) methods of birth control. In order to comprehend this issue, it is necessary to examine the attitudes of the poor toward sexual behavior.

Kinsey has documented that lower-income people prefer intercourse in the dark, with their clothes on.[6] Nakedness, both due to crowded living conditions and greater inhibition, is frowned upon. Masturbation is negatively regarded in low-income culture, and apparently practiced less. Foreplay also occurs less often, Kinsey says.

Moreover, low-income people do not talk about sex in the intellectualized, open fashion common in middle-class families. The organized group meetings sponsored by Planned Parent-

[3] Lee Rainwater, *And the Poor Get Children,* Chicago, Quadrangle Books, 1960, p. 24.

[4] *Ibid.,* p. 25.

[5] An investigation of the family size preferences of nonwhite parents seems to show that nonwhite wives want *fewer* children than the white wives in the sample—the average number desired by the nonwhite sample was 2.9 as against 3.3 by the white wives. (Adelaide C. Hill and Frederick S. Jaffee, "Negro Fertility and Family Size Preferences," in K. Clark and T. Parsons, eds., *The American Negro,* Houghton Mifflin, Boston, p. 11.) Other studies where comparisons of racial groups are made seem also to indicate that Negro respondents consistently expressed the wish to have fewer additional children than the white respondents. (Robert H. Browning and L. L. Parks, "Childbearing Aspirations of Public Health Maternity Patients," *American Journal of Public Health,* Vol. 54, No. 11, November 1964, p. 1832.)

[6] Alfred C. Kinsey, *et al., Sexual Behavior in the Human Male,* Philadelphia, Saunders, 1948.

hood might be somewhat alien to low-income people. Here, a leader typically describes to a mixed audience of men and women the various techniques in a frank, straightforward manner, and discussion follows. From what we know of low-income traditions, this would seem to be an atypical experience. Is it possible in the light of this population's sexual attitudes to have group instruction in mixed groups, or must this be done more in a one-to-one and sex-segregated fashion?

In light of the apparently negative attitude toward masturbation among low-income individuals, a technique such as the diaphragm, which involves touching of the organs, might be resisted. This device in addition requires a privacy not always available in low-income homes. The diaphragm also requires a planning of the evening's sexuality, as it were. The diaphragm and the condom may interfere both physically and psychologically with the direct, "natural," motion of the act.* Middle-class people may also object to these mechnical contraceptive devices for this reason. However, they have coping mechanisms, or styles, which allow for these rituals. In addition, they can even utilize these contraceptive procedures as part of the foreplay, as has been suggested by birth control expert Dr. Alan Guttmacher:

> One objection (to the use of the condom) is that love play must be interrupted to put the condom on, but imaginative couples have found this to present no difficulties; they usually make this part of the pleasurable preparations for intercourse with the wife making the placement as a signal that she is ready.[7]

However, this is sexual advice which would probably fall on deaf ears among the low-income population where foreplay is typically not an integral part of the sexual act. Guttmacher currently recognizes the inapplicability of this kind of approach to the low-income group. Referring to the low utilization of Planned Parenthood clinics by the poor, he states:

* This is not to imply that low-income sexuality is characterized by great freedom and spontaneity. As a matter of fact, as Rainwater *et al.* note in *Workingman's Wife,* lt is frequently quite inhibited and laden with traditional superstitious attitudes.

[7] Alan F. Guttmacher, *The Complete Book of Birth Control,* rev. ed., New York, Ballantine Books, 1963, p. 40.

The failure of these clinics to attract and help a substantial portion of the population can be accounted for, in the light of recent experiences, by the fact that the contraceptive methods they generally offer are ill-suited to the life circumstances of most poor people. . . . Often they (the women) lack both the privacy and the knowledge required to employ the most effective vaginal methods of contraception; some, for example, unaware of the existence of the cervix, are afraid the diaphragm will be "lost inside." For their part, the men are often highly insistent on their "rights" to coitus, and impatient with any delay or physical obstruction. Thus, contraceptive techniques that coincide with the very act of coitus . . . may become extremely problematic. . . . Meanwhile, abortion, a "coitus-independent" method of birth regulation, commonly flourishes despite the health hazards and legal risks when it is performed clandestinely.[8]

The elaborate monthly records, as well as the daily temperature taking required of the rhythm method, are much more consistent with the orientation of the middle-class person. In low-income homes, with the many pressures, such a technique would be less congenial. In addition, limited education might be expected to make the keeping of these records more difficult.

The oral contraceptive method does meet the cultural needs in that it is, to use Guttmacher's phrase, completely *coitus-independent*. Also, it is appropriate in other respects. "Since it does not involve the genitals physically or psychologically, it can be talked about freely by these women who, contrary to stereotypes, are often prudish and embarrassed to acknowledge their own sexuality, much less to accept and recommend a contraceptive."[9]

The IUD, or any method of permanent contraception, would appear to have the least problems. One of its advantages is that it does not require the planning of the evening's sexuality; it is completely coitus-independent.*

[8] Steven Polgar and Alan F. Guttmacher, "A New Chapter in Family Planning," *Columbia University Forum*, Vol. 8, No. 3, Fall 1965, p. 34.
[9] E. James Lieberman, "Preventive Psychiatry and Family Planning," *Journal of Marriage and the Family*, Vol. 16, No. 4, November 1964, p. 475.
* On the other hand, low-income people may have disturbing attitudes about a foreign body which is constantly in them. With the less educated,

THE CULTURE OF POVERTY:
AN INAPPLICABLE CONCEPT

The striking discrepancy between the preference for small families and the fact of larger-than-average families among a large segment of the population has most commonly been described as stemming from "insufficient or ambivalent motivation" with respect to family planning. It seemed indeed reasonable to interpret the observed failures in effective contraceptive practice in this fashion. During the past decade, however, demonstration projects and large-scale action programs have challenged this academic interpretation along with other, less sympathetic labels suggested by indignant politicians or taxpayers.[10]

A theory has evolved which states that "members of the lower socio-economic groups are less likely to utilize existing health facilities or to take part in preventive health programs."[11] This view derives from a "culture of poverty" concept which sees the poor as unable to plan, pessimistic, and difficult to reach in regard to health practices. This "hard core," "medically deprived" group is supposedly resistant to change in attitudes and behavior in regard to health, disease, and medical care.[12]

---

particularly, the mechanics regarding where the device is located and what it does to prevent conception are mysterious. The device is a real magnet for superstition. With more educated persons, the behavior would probably be organized more readily around the new knowledge; education would enable them to understand the process and define it accordingly. The low-income person might be more likely to respond negatively to the strange shape of the coil or other intrauterine device, and be suspicious about its presence in the body. In spite of their superstitions, however, the extreme effectiveness and ease of this method does provoke a response among this group. A little-advertised contraception clinic at Sloane Hospital for Women (Columbia University-Presbyterian Medical Center) has been widely utilized by medically indigent women coming for maternity services; in 1963 almost one-third of the women who delivered there chose the IUD. (See Polgar and Guttmacher, *op. cit.*, pp. 34-35.)

[10] Gitta Meier, "Research and Action Programs in Human Fertility Control: A Review of the Literature," *Social Work,* Vol. 11, No. 3, July 1966, p. 46.

[11] Edward A. Suchman, *Sociology and the Field of Public Health,* New York, Russell Sage Foundation, 1963, p. 64.

[12] Edward A. Suchman, "Medical Deprivation," *American Journal of Orthopsychiatry,* July 1966, Vol. XXXVI, No. 4, pp. 665-671.

For many, if not most, individuals, especially those with limited social horizons and immediate needs, the rewards of preventive health behavior are too remote to carry much weight. The negative consequences of not acting are not real and dire enough to arouse the energy required to do something out of the ordinary, such as taking part in a public health program.[13]

Within the field of family planning, the theory of cultural resistance cites the low-income individual's lack of a "futuristic outlook"[14] and sees this as mitigating against adequate use of birth control devices. "The middle class person tends to be more planful than the lower class individual, who usually lives for today, is not optimistic about the future, and feels that his efforts will bear little fruit."[15] Rainwater sees this cultural trait as the reason behind the inconsistent and ineffective family planning patterns of the poor.

They (the poor) tend to regard thought and planning as painful activities to be engaged in only under the pressure of great necessity. Even then, they are not optimistic, since they often feel that the best they can do will not be sufficient to overcome adversity—one may be spared unpleasantness by good fortune, one may be "lucky," but one cannot be personally successful against difficulty. Such a world view and way of thinking about oneself in the world are not conducive to effective planning. Indeed, they tend to discourage planning and the hope it implies, lest one court disappointment.[16]

In its most extreme form this thesis of cultural deprivation and its effect on the utilization of health services states that:

The effective control of fertility requires individual initiative and sustained effort. People who do not really believe that it is possible for them to improve conditions of life

[13] Paul Cornely and Stanley Bigman, "Cultural Considerations in Changing Health Attitudes," mimeographed, 1961, as quoted in Suchman, *Sociology and the Field of Public Health,* p. 84.

[14] Florence Kluckhohn and Fred L. Strodtbeck, *et al., Variations in Value Orientation,* New York, Harper & Row, 1961.

[15] Sidney Furie, "Birth Control and the Lower Class Unmarried Mother," *Social Work,* Vol. 11, No. 1, January 1966, p. 45.

[16] Rainwater, *op. cit.,* p. 53.

for themselves or their children will not undertake a radically new venture or put forth the sustained effort required for success in this undertaking. Where hope is weak, contraception will be absent or ineffective.[17]

But perhaps the thesis of cultural resistance to contraception on the part of the poor was after the fact. Because our public policy was so confused and because services, where available, were fragmented, inconveniently located, inhumanely delivered, and bureaucratically organized, the lack of adequate family planning among the poor was incorrectly seen as reflecting an inability to make use of modern health practices. Because the middle class had little difficulty in limiting their families, one tended to view the problem as culture based, overlooking the greater availability of services and information to this stratum. With the lack of services and educational programs among the poor regarding the proper use of contraceptive measures, there arose a cycle of skepticism and contraceptive failures, which Rainwater documents so well. "This 'chain reaction' of failure with conventional techniques may have been a major cause of the traditional lagging interest of many impoverished families."[18] With the improved technology provided by coitus-independent methods (the pill and the IUD) and the beginnings of truly available and accessible services for these groups, the picture changes.

It is becoming increasingly clear that the availability of birth control facilities (clinics, etc.) within the lower socioeconomic groups rapidly increases utilization of these services. Several studies have shown that with availability of coitus-independent devices there is continued high utilization of the services. A pilot project in Mecklenburg County, North Carolina, begun in 1960, used 264 women volunteers (married, previously married, and single women who had borne children) who were public welfare clients, and made oral contraceptives available to them. (Ninety percent were Negro, 10 percent were white. The mean age was 29, mean grade completed in high school was 9, mean number of children

[17] Frank Lorimer, "Issues in Population Policy," in Philip Hauser, ed., *The Population Dilemma*, Englewood Cliffs, N.J., Prentice-Hall, 1963, pp. 148-149.
[18] Rainwater, *op. cit.*, p. 53.

was 4.8. Of the women working, 89 percent held unskilled positions, largely as domestics. The majority live in over-crowded, depressed area housing.) [19] After two years 223 of these individuals were still active in the program. But perhaps more significant, other women in the county virtually began "knocking the doors down to be referred to the 'pill clinic.' "[20]

It might be added that the response to this service was a great surprise to the officials and professionals involved; the welfare staff, doctors, nurses, social workers, felt that these economically and socially deprived women "would not be able to follow the regimen necessary to make successful use of the pills."[21] The Mecklenburg study is especially significant in this context, for these patients were using the oral contracep-tive, a method perhaps requiring the utmost planning and systematic organization of any of the available methods—one pill a day for twenty successive days.

The Chicago Planned Parenthood conducted a study in-volving more than 14,000 patients using oral contraceptives: 83 percent of the patients were nonwhite, slightly less than half had not completed high school, and one out of six were welfare recipients. It was found that between 70 and 83 per-cent continued to take the pills in the required manner for thirty months after they came to the clinic.[22] "This is an astonishingly high retention rate for *any* procedure requiring continuous self-administration of medication and says some-thing about the readiness of the poor to respond to well-conceived, energetically-delivered voluntary programs employ-ing coitus-independent methods."[23]

It is important to note here, however, that these studies

[19] Elizabeth C. Corkey, "A Family Planning Program for the Low-Income Family," *Journal of Marriage and the Family,* Vol. 26, No. 4, November 1964, pp. 478-480.

[20] Wallace Kuralt, "Mecklenburg County: A Pilot Pill Project for Welfare Recipients," in *Birth Control Services in Tax Supported Hospitals, Health Departments and Welfare Agencies,* New York, Planned Parenthood—World Population, pp. 38-39.

[21] *Ibid.,* pp. 38-39.

[22] Richard Frank and Christopher Rietze, "Acceptance of an Oral Con-traceptive Program in a Large Metropolitan Area," *American Journal of Obstetrics and Gynecology,* Vol. 93, No. 122, September 1, 1965.

[23] Frederick S. Jaffee, "Family Planning, Public Policy and Intervention Strategy," mimeographed, 1965.

were attempting to reach a selective sample of the poor: the women were volunteers in both the Mecklenburg and the Chicago projects. These, then, were perhaps the most receptive elements of the poor. Rainwater's thesis may still be valid for the nonvolunteers in the low-income group: the "sporadic or careless users."[24] The sporadic users are composed of couples "with some desire to limit their families but who for a variety of reasons are unable to practice contraception effectively even though they may have considerable knowledge about various methods."[25] But even reaching a small and self-selected percentage of the poor resulted in a *diffusion* effect, as it were. In the Mecklenburg study hundreds of other women, hearing of the service, asked to become part of the program. The availability of the services, therefore, in a comprehensive program, results in the spread of utilization beyond the original volunteer sample.

Writing about the high response to the new programs such as Mecklenburg, Chicago, etc., Hill and Jaffee succinctly capture the differential character of these programs:

The most successful demonstration projects have, to one degree or another, been considerably different from the kind of medical care which impoverished Negroes normally receive. Instead of compelling patients to sit for hours on end in dingy waiting rooms, appointments are often scheduled (as in private practice) and efforts are made to offer a bright and cheerful atmosphere. Many clinics are located in the heart of impoverished neighborhoods, not halfway across town, and sessions may be scheduled at night and other unusual times to fit patients' needs. Staff members are urged to refrain from imposing their attitudes and values upon patients and nonprofessional workers have been employed to interpret to potential patients how family planning can help them to realize their desires about family size. Baby sitting services are sometimes provided. Fees are adjusted to what the patient can afford. And perhaps most significant, clinics are not segregated by color.[26]

[24] Rainwater, *op. cit.*, p. 29.
[25] *Ibid.*, p. 43.
[26] Hill and Jaffee, *op. cit.*, p. 13.

THE SIGNIFICANCE OF
THE NONPROFESSIONAL

Rainwater observes that a highly significant new development in the field of family planning among the poor is the
use of nonprofessionals or neighborhood residents.[27] Here a
cultural approach to the problem is built in, as it were, by
using individuals from a socioeconomic background similar
to the recipients' as dispensers of the information, able to
communicate in the appropriate cultural idiom. The *New
York Times* recently reported a highly successful experiment
conducted by Bogue and Palmore in the rural South (thirteen
Black Belt counties in southern Alabama with a heavy rural
Negro poulation and eight Appalachian Mountain counties
of eastern Kentucky inhabited largely by rural whites) using
all the modern contraceptive techniques on a population
which many feel is one of the most difficult to reach.

Success apparently depends on a variety of factors. However, one key seems to be the use of local residents, instead
of polished, professional outsiders, to spread information
by word of mouth. . . . The experimenters have hired a
"family planning educator" in each Black Belt county.
The educator is a Negro woman who is widely known,
liked and respected in the community, a person able to
talk informally with the women visiting the health
clinics.[28]

The Planned Parenthood Federation is also utilizing nonprofessional workers in an action-research project in New
York City, which uses community centers as its base. "In three
of the centers, nonprofessional 'neighborhood workers' are
attempting to stimulate interest in the service by organizing
'coffee sips' where family planning is discussed in informal

[27] Lee Rainwater, "The Lower Class: Health, Illness and Medical Institutions." Background paper prepared for a study of medical facilities
planning conducted by Anselm L. Strauss for the Institute of Policy
Studies, March 1965, p. 22.

[28] *New York Times,* January 7, 1966, and June 25, 1966. See also Donald
J. Bogue and James A. Palmore, "The Chicago Fertility Control Experiments: Some Preliminary Findings." Paper presented at the Annual Meeting of the American Public Health Association, New York, New York,
October 1964.

BIRTH CONTROL, CULTURE, AND THE POOR § 111

groups."[29] It is unlikely that these workers would present the information in the more clinically antiseptic manner often employed by the professional staff, which encountered resistance on the part of the local residents.

Bringing these services into the neighborhoods of the poor, into storefronts staffed by nonprofessionals, could constitute a breakthrough. With this approach we are bypassing a cultural analysis, or more accurately, we are incorporating the culture via the nonprofessionals who function as a link with the poor. With the perfected birth control technology which uses methods less likely to encounter resistance on cultural grounds from the poor, the maximum use of birth control facilities might be forthcoming.

The evidence indicates that low-income people desire to control the size of their families. Their failure to do so in the past was probably related to the lack of available birth control services and to the fact that the only techniques available were coitus-connected. These techniques appear to be antithetical to the sexual attitudes and traditions of the poor.

With the advent of coitus-independent measures, and the effort to make them available to the poor in a humane, well-organized, neighborhood-based fashion, utilization by low-income people is changing dramatically. The culture-of-poverty thesis which attributes nonuse of birth control information by the poor to apathy, a lack of planning, and a nonfuturistic orientation, seems to be highly doubtful in light of the new evidence.

Family planning is not a panacea for all the problems of poverty and dependence, nor is it a substitute for massive social programs to enable (the) impoverished . . . to obtain jobs, increase income levels, enlarge educational opportunities and otherwise improve their living conditions. But the reduction of poverty and dependency will not be slowed significantly, no matter how comprehensive these programs, unless the poor, white and nonwhite, are also able to have only the number of children they want. In the spectrum of urgently needed programs, family planning is one which is achievable relatively quickly and easily. With modern methods, we have suf-

[29] Polgar and Guttmacher, *op. cit.,* p. 35.

ficient knowledge and technology; it is a relatively simple and inexpensive aspect of medical care; the number of patients to be served is quite limited; and most important, the poor have shown considerable readiness of response to this service. It is not necessary to remould basic attitudes or develop new aspirations among (the) impoverished . . ., but to provide the means of realizing aspirations they already have.[30]

[30] Hill and Jaffee, *op. cit.,* p. 17.

CONCLUSION

The three major antipoverty strategies discussed—Cloward-Piven, Alinsky's local conflict model and the New Careers design—all contribute significant elements to a comprehensive antipoverty attack. Alinsky reminds us of the significance of conflict and power and brings to national attention the importance of local consumer involvement in decision making. Moreover, he recognizes that conflict and organization are crucial in order to develop the power of the poor and local control. These concepts have been well absorbed by the developing consumer demands for decentralization, neighborhood control and black power. They are crucial ingredients in the emerging antipoverty demands of the black and other minority groups in America. This despite the fact that the Alinsky model itself rarely addresses itself toward a national program. The new concern for decentralization is reflected in the rapidly proliferating neighborhood service-center movement, which is discussed in chapter eight.

The Cloward-Piven welfare rights strategy focuses again on consumer involvement and the rights of the consumer. It levels a powerful attack on the welfare anti-service system which has functioned to prevent people from moving out of poverty and encumbered them with a whole series of requirements that function to maintain them further in the cycle of poverty. If the welfare rights movement combines with the job-creation movement in the United States, a major anti-poverty thrust will emerge.

The New Careers approach attempts to move people out of poverty via jobs and a career ladder which will enable them to become professionals, administrators, and so on. The New Careers design attempts to combine both a legislative strategy and a movement strategy. Thus far the legislative impact inside the system has been greater than that of the movement outside the system. If New Careers captures the imagination of the nonprofessionals, it could then organize together with the professional supporters and unite with other movements including the welfare rights groups to launch a large-scale antipoverty attack.

ABOUT THE AUTHOR

FRANK RIESSMAN is Director of the New Careers Train-
ing Laboratory and The New Careers Development
Center, and is Professor of Educational Sociology at
New York University. He was with Mobilization for
Youth and was formerly the Director of the Lincoln
Hospital Mental Health Aide Program.

Dr. Riessman is the author of *Up From Poverty,*
with Hermine Popper, and *Social Class and Social
Policy,* with S. M. Miller. As well, he has written *The
Culturally Deprived Child,* and (with A. Pearl) *New
Careers for the Poor,* and *Mental Health of the Poor*
(with J. Cohen and A. Pearl).

In addition, Dr. Riessman is an activist and leader
in the antipoverty movement, and a frequent con-
tributor to popular and professional journals.

DATE DUE